Glendale Library, Arts & Culture Dept.

D0746517

English Made Easy

VOLUME TWO

A NEW **ESL** APPROACH

Learning English **Through Pictures**

Jonathan Crichton and Pieter Koster

TUTTLE Publishing

Tokyo | Rutland, Vermont | Singapore

428.24 CRI

Contents

ABOUT TUTTLE
"Books to Span the East and West"

Our core mission at Tuttle Publishing is to create books which bring people together one page at a time. Tuttle was founded in 1832 in the small New England town of Rutland, Vermont (USA). Our fundamental values remain as strong today as they were then—to publish best-in-class books informing the English-speaking world about the countries and peoples of Asia. The world has become a smaller place today and Asia's economic, cultural and political influence has expanded, yet the need for meaningful dialogue and information about this diverse region has never been greater. Since 1948, Tuttle has been a leader in publishing books on the cultures, arts, cuisines, languages and literatures of Asia. Our authors and photographers have won numerous awards and Tuttle has published thousands of books on subjects ranging from martial arts to paper crafts. We welcome you to explore the wealth of information available on Asia at **www.tuttlepublishing.com**.

Published by Tuttle Publishing, an imprint of Periplus Editions (HK) Ltd

www.tuttlepublishing.com

Copyright © 2015 Periplus Editions (HK) Ltd

All rights reserved. No part of this publication may be reproduced or utilized in any form or by any means, electronic or mechanical, including photocopying, recording, or by any information storage and retrieval system, without prior written permission from the publisher.

ISBN 978-0-8048-4646-2 (British Edition)
ISBN 978-0-8048-4525-0 (American Edition)

18 17 16 15
10 9 8 7 6 5 4 3 2 1
Printed in Malaysia   1512TW

Distributed by:

North America, Latin America & Europe
Tuttle Publishing
364 Innovation Drive
North Clarendon, VT 05759-9436 U.S.A.
Tel: 1 (802) 773-8930
Fax: 1 (802) 773-6993
info@tuttlepublishing.com
www.tuttlepublishing.com

Japan
Tuttle Publishing
Yaekari Building, 3rd Floor
5-4-12 Osaki, Shinagawa-ku, Tokyo 141-0032
Tel: (81) 3 5437-0171
Fax: (81) 3 5437-0755
sales@tuttle.co.jp
www.tuttle.co.jp

Asia Pacific
Berkeley Books Pte. Ltd.
61 Tai Seng Avenue, #02-12, Singapore 534167
Tel: (65) 6280-1330
Fax: (65) 6280-6290
inquiries@periplus.com.sg
www.periplus.com

TUTTLE PUBLISHING® is a registered trademark of Tuttle Publishing, a division of Periplus Editions (HK) Ltd.

Preface

In an increasingly international world, being able to communicate in English is nowadays a necessity in social, professional and business life. Competence in English creates an increasing range of business, travel and leisure opportunities, opening doors to international communication.

This book is a breakthrough in English language learning—imaginatively exploiting how pictures and text can work together to create understanding and help learners learn more productively.

English Made Easy gives learners easy access to the vocabulary, grammar and functions of English as it is actually used in a comprehensive range of social situations. Self-guided students and classroom learners alike will be delighted by the way they are helped to progress easily from one unit to the next, using the combinations of pictures and text to discover for themselves how English works.

The *English Made Easy* method is based on a thorough understanding of language structure and how language is successfully learned. The authors are experienced English language teachers with strong backgrounds in language analysis and language learning. The *English Made Easy* team is confident that the books represent a significant development in English language learning.

—Professor Christopher N. Candlin, Macquarie University

Introduction

This is a book that keeps its promise. It makes learning English easy.

People today learn English for a wide variety of purposes. You may use English in your work, live in an English-speaking country, or be planning to visit one. Whatever your purpose, *English Made Easy* is a perfect way to learn basic skills in English language communication.

English Made Easy does not teach grammar. It teaches you how to use English. Grammar informs the way that the book is structured, but the authors believe that, especially at beginner level, new students do not need to clutter their learning with grammatical labels and rules. They learn by observing, discovering and practicing how language is used.

English Made Easy uses the universal language of pictures to present language in the contexts in which it is used. Students learn the meaning of what is written by studying how language is used in the pictures. Real life social situations are broken down into their simplest parts so that students quickly see how the language works and relate it to their own needs. It's actually fun!

English Made Easy can be used by an individual student or by a group of learners in a conversation group or classroom with a teacher. Because students don't need to know the grammar before they start, it is easy to guide learners through the pages of *English Made Easy* or for learners to use it for self study.

The first page of each unit outlines what you can expect to learn from the unit. It includes word lists and a note about the grammar in the unit. This note is for information only and need not be learned by the student. Some of the units also contain brief fill-in exercises, and every fifth unit provides practice activities for revision and extension. Answers are provided. The index refers students to the unit in which the word is introduced.

To all our learners, wherever you are and however you use this book, we wish you every success!

—Jonathan Crichton and Pieter Koster

UNIT 1: Here's a letter for you.

In this unit you will learn the following:

- How to talk about family members
- How to communicate with friends

Here are the words you will learn to use:

airmail	cat	envelope	invitation	off	put	to
all	chair	fax	land	on	quickly	uncle
aunt	close	from	letter	open	sister-in-law	want
bill	cousin	grandfather	letterbox	parcel	sofa	
brother-in-law	daughter-in-law	grandmother	nephew	postcard	son-in-law	
card	email	holidays	niece	postman	stamp	

Here are some phrases you will learn to use:

lay the table	butter the toast	clear the table	look forward to	depart from	hurry up
make the toast	pass the milk	load the dishwasher	arrive at	take off	

Here are some sentences you will practice:

Here's a postcard for you. It's for you. The cat is off the sofa.

Could you open the door, please. The dog is on the chair.

1 This is the Benson family.

2 This is Jim and Peggy.

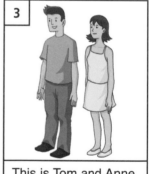

3 This is Tom and Anne.

4 They live at 2 Richmond Street.

Grammar tips:
The new structures in this unit are imperatives, prepositions and paired verbs.

The Benson Family

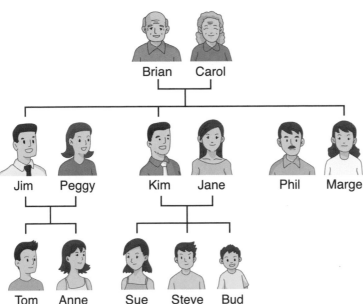

1. Jim is Anne's father.
2. Anne is Jim's daughter.
3. Tom is Anne's brother.
4. Marge is Jim's sister.
5. Kim is Jim's brother.
6. Brian is Jim's father.
7. Brian is Tom's grandfather.
8. Carol is Tom's grandmother.
9. Marge is Carol's daughter.
10. Peggy is Carol's daughter-in-law.
11. Kim is Anne's uncle.
12. Marge is Anne's aunt.
13. Sue is Anne's cousin.
14. Anne is Sue's cousin.
15. Sue is Jim's niece.
16. Steve is Jim's nephew.
17. Jane is Jim's sister-in-law.
18. Kim is Peggy's brother-in-law.
19. Phil is Carol's son-in law.

The Taylor Family

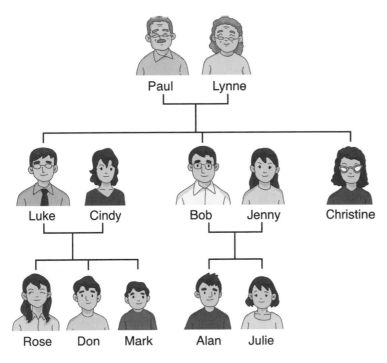

1. Bob is Julie's _____ .
2. Julie is Bob's _____ .
3. Alan is Julie's _____ .
4. Lynne is Alan's _____ .
5. Cindy is Bob's _____ .
6. Paul is Bob's _____ .
7. Jenny is Lynne's _____ .
8. Luke is Bob's _____ .
9. Christine is Lynne's _____ .
10. Rose is Julie's _____ .
11. Luke is Julie's _____ .
12. Christine is Julie's _____ .
13. Christine is Bob's _____ .
14. Julie is Rose's _____ .
15. Paul is Alan's _____ .
16. Don is Bob's _____ .
17. Rose is Bob's _____ .
18. Luke is Jenny's _____ .

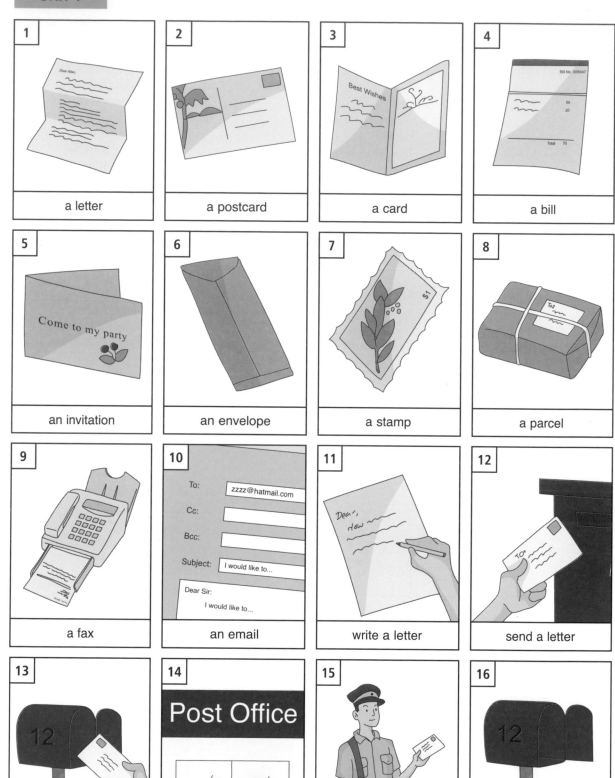

1 — a letter	2 — a postcard
3 — a card	4 — a bill
5 — an invitation	6 — an envelope
7 — a stamp	8 — a parcel
9 — a fax	10 — an email
11 — write a letter	12 — send a letter
13 — get a letter	14 — a post office
15 — a postman	16 — a letterbox

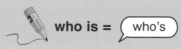

A postcard from Andy and Janet

1

a dog

2

a chair

3

The dog is on the chair.

4

The dog is off the chair.

5

a cat

6

a sofa

7

The cat is on the sofa.

8

The cat is off the sofa.

9

Don't put the dog on the chair!

10

Put a stamp on the envelope.

1

arrive at the hotel

2

arrive at the hotel at two o'clock

3

depart from the hotel

4

depart from the hotel at nine o'clock

5

land at the airport

6

take off from the airport

1

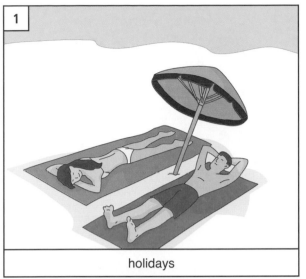

holidays

2

looking forward to holidays

3

fast   slow

4

Hurry up!

5

Can I have more, please?

He's got one grape.

6

Can I have more, please?

He's got some grapes.

7

He's got all the grapes.

13

The Bensons

1

This is the Benson's house.
The postman is putting a letter in the letterbox.

2

Here's a letter for you, Jim.

3

Hurry up! Open it! When are they coming?

Anne wants Jim to open the letter quickly.

4

Dear Jim and Peggy,

Thanks for your invitation to stay at your new house. Sue is looking forward to seeing Anne. Our plane arrives at 8 o'clock on Thursday next week. It's flight number 412. Can you meet us at the airport?

Look forward to seeing you all.

Sincerely,
Kim

5

Thursday next week.

6

We can meet them at the airport, can't we?

Yes, of course. I'll ring them.

7

Lay the table, please, Anne. I'll make the toast.

8

9 Butter the toast, please, Tom.

10 Pass the milk, please, Anne.

11 Clear the table, load the dishwasher and let's go.

12

13 It's a quarter to eight. We're early.

14 ARRIVALS   FLIGHT 421 : LANDED

15 ARRIVALS   It's half past eight. Where are Kim and Sue?

UNIT 2: Let's check the flight number again.

In this unit you will learn the following:
- How to talk about time
- How to report events
- How to check details

Here are the words you will learn to use:

accident	bored	exciting	interesting	ring	surprised	tiring
again	boring	frightened	never	say	surprising	trophy
always	check	frightening	once	sometimes	tell	twice
bell	excited	interested	right (not wrong)	student	tired	wrong

Here are some phrases you will learn to use:

a bit   three times   be late   be early   on time   a long time

Here are some sentences you will practice:

Tell John I'll be late.   He said he'll be late.   Shopping is tiring.

What did you say?   You said you were working late.   She is tired.

She said she would meet us at eleven.   The bus is late.   This bus is always on time.

Grammar tips:

The new structures used in this unit are reported speech, present and past participles used as adjectives, and adverbs of frequency

16

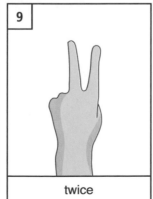

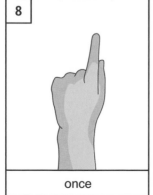

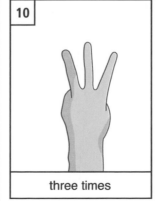

once

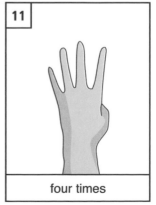

twice

three times

four times

will not = won't

1

short

long

This string is too short.

This string is too long.

2

How long have you been here?

I've been here for two hours.

3

How long has it been there?

A long time.

4

Next train 4:15

The next train won't come for a long time.

5

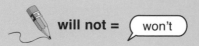

Goodbye, Harry.

Goodbye, Rick.

6

I haven't seen him for a long time.

7

Hello, Dick. It's good to see you again.

8

Hello, Harry. It's been a long time, hasn't it? How have you been?

Good, good. How have you been?

9

I'm good now. I was sick for a long time but now I'm better again.

That's good. I'm glad you're better.

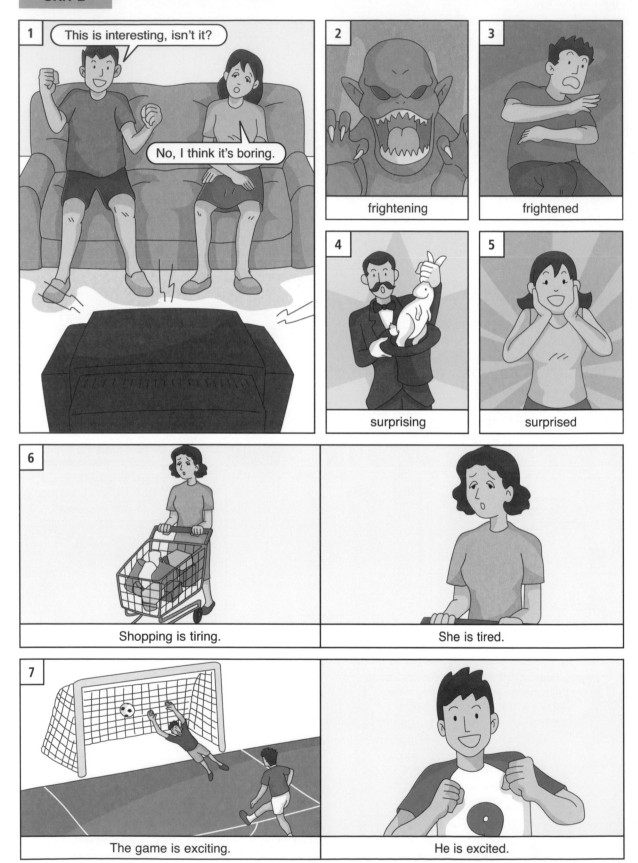

1

The teacher is boring.
The student is bored.

2

The teacher is very boring.
The student is very bored.

3

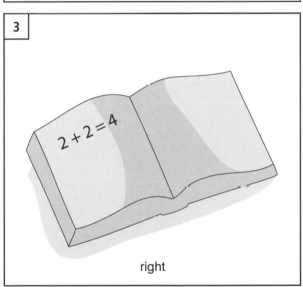

$2 + 2 = 4$

right

4

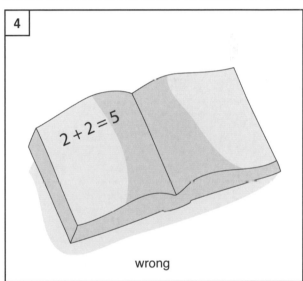

$2 + 2 = 5$

wrong

5

Mr Willis?

Yes, that's right.

Ken Willis

6

Is that 9494956?

No, sorry, wrong number.
This is 9494965.

The Bensons

The Benson family arrives at the airport again.

UNIT 3: It's a goal!

In this unit you will learn the following:

- How to talk about accommodation
- How to talk about quantities

Here are the words you will learn to use:

almost	bedroom	equal	goal	upstairs	seat	through
another	bird	fence	half	mess	share	toilet
back	dining room	front	hamburger	money	shed	tunnel
backyard	double bed	garage	into	path	single bed	unequal
balcony	downstairs	garden	kitchen	roof	tandem	with
bathroom	enough	gate	living room	sauce	tidy	without

Here are some phrases you will learn to use:

not enough   too much   lots of   out of   there is   there are

Here are some sentences you will practice:

There are three birds on the roof.

Share the cake with your sister.

There's a train going into the tunnel.

This is enough money.

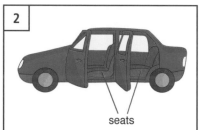

1

a car

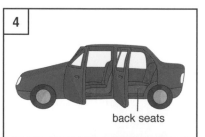

2

seats

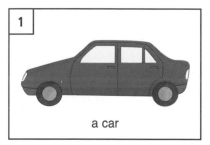

3

front seats

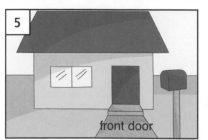

4

back seats

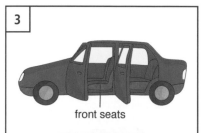

5

front door

6

back door

Grammar tips:

The new structures in this unit are quantifiers and prepositions

1
a bird

2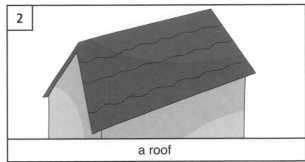
a roof

3
There are three birds on the roof.

4
Now there are two birds on the roof.

5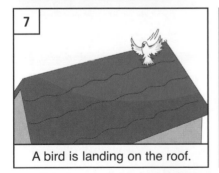
Now there is one bird on the roof.

6
Now there are no birds on the roof.

7
A bird is landing on the roof.

8
Another bird is landing on the roof.

9
Lots of birds are landing on the roof.

10
It's a goal!

It's another goal!

And another goal!!

1

one cake

2

two boys

3

share the cake

4

Share the cake with your sister.

5

half

half each

6

equal

7

unequal

1

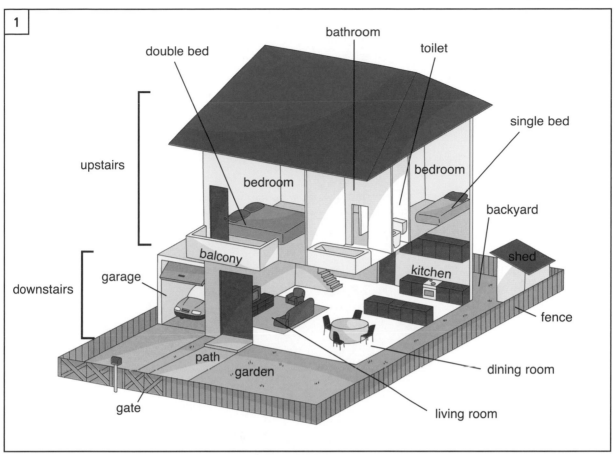

- double bed
- bathroom
- toilet
- single bed
- upstairs
- bedroom
- bedroom
- backyard
- single bed
- downstairs
- garage
- balcony
- shed
- kitchen
- fence
- path
- garden
- dining room
- gate
- living room

2

a tidy living room	a party in the living room	a mess in the living room
Tidy up.	tidying the living room	a tidy living room again

29

1

money

This watch costs $50.00.

This is enough money.

Not enough money.

Almost enough money.

Too much money.

Here's your change.

Not enough change.

2

a tunnel

There's a train going into the tunnel.

There's a train going through the tunnel.

There's a train coming out of the tunnel.

1

a hamburger

2

a hamburger with sauce

3

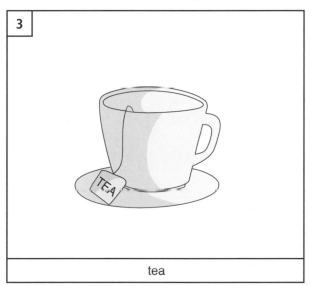

tea

4

tea without milk

5

a tandem

6

with his friend

7

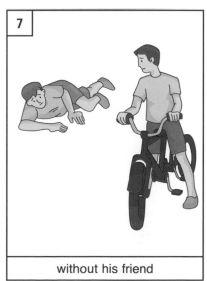

without his friend

The Bensons

7 Here's the bathroom and toilet. There's another bathroom upstairs.

8 It's a lovely house, Jim. I like it.

Thank you. We like it too, don't we, Peggy?

9 Yes, we do. And here's the kitchen and the dining room is through that door.

10 So there are two bedrooms downstairs and one more upstairs.

Yes, that's right. And there are two bathrooms, one upstairs and one downstairs.

11 And here's the backyard.

You've got a big shed for your garden tools.

12 It's a lovely view, isn't it?

Oh, there's a balcony, too!

UNIT 4: I want a chocolate bar!

In this unit you will learn the following:
- How to make plans

Here are the words you will learn to use:

anniversary	birthday	excellent	trip	while	zoo
around	chocolate bar	stars	walk	world	

Here are some phrases you will learn to use:

around here   one year old

Here are some sentences you will practice:

What are you doing on Sunday?	Have you been to Australia?	You were in Alaska while I was in Hawaii.
It's his birthday.	It's around here somewhere.	This hotel is good.

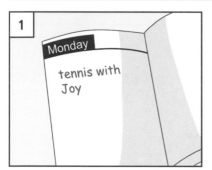

1 Monday — tennis with Joy

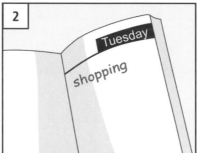

2 Tuesday — shopping

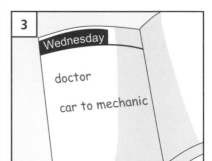

3 Wednesday — doctor, car to mechanic

4 Thursday — art gallery with Alison

5 Friday — party at John's house

6 Saturday — write letters, work in garden

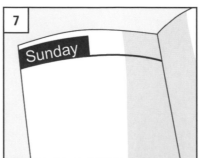

7 Sunday

Grammar tips:

The new structures in this unit are present continuous tense with future meaning, and present perfect tense.

1 I'm very busy this week. On Monday I'm playing tennis with Joy. On Tuesday I'm going shopping. On Wednesday I'm seeing the doctor and taking the car to the mechanic. On Thursday I'm going to the art gallery with Alison. On Friday I'm going to a party at John's house. And on Saturday I'm writing some letters and working in the garden.

2 What are you doing on Sunday?

3 I don't know. I think I'll sleep all day!

1

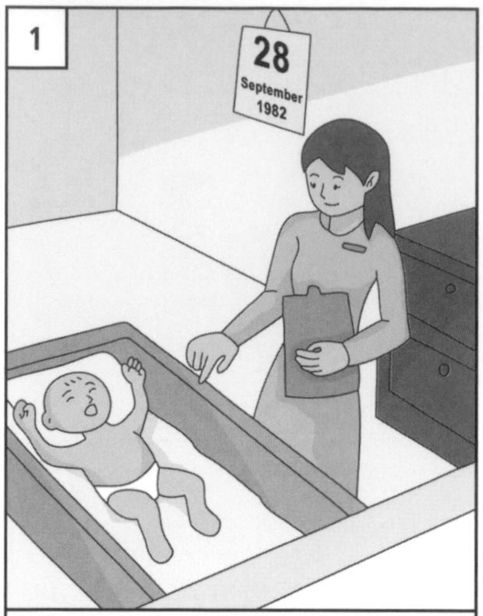

28th September 1982

2

It's his first birthday.
He's one year old today.

3

It's his second birthday.
He's two years old today.

4

I'm ten!

It's his birthday.
He's ten years old today.

5

I'm 21 today.

It's his birthday. He's 21 today.

6

Is it my birthday today?

Yes, it is.
You're 90 today.

7

4th August 2000

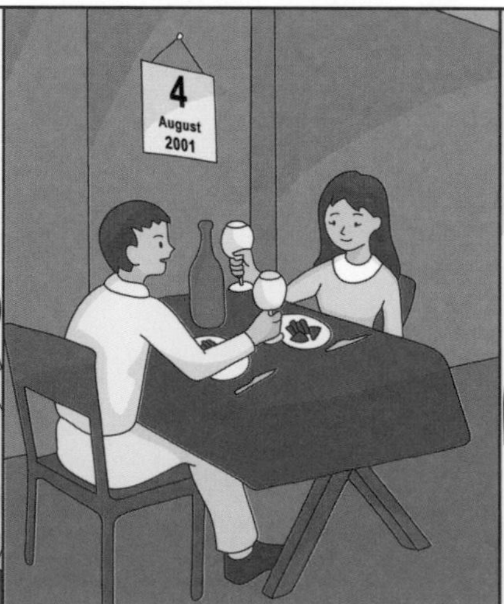

It's their first anniversary.

It's their fiftieth anniversary.

1

around the book

2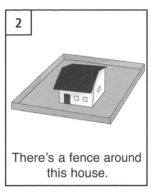

There's a fence around this house.

3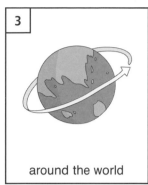

around the world

4

I'm going for a trip around the world.

5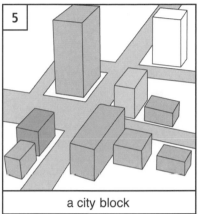

a city block

6

walk

7

walk around the block

8

Where's my book?

Here.

9

Where's my book?

It's around here somewhere.

10

Where are my glasses?

I don't know. They're around here somewhere.

11

Do you like this restaurant?

Yes, I think it's the best restaurant around here.

a chocolate bar

The Bensons

The Benson's are having dinner with their guests, Kim and Sue.

42

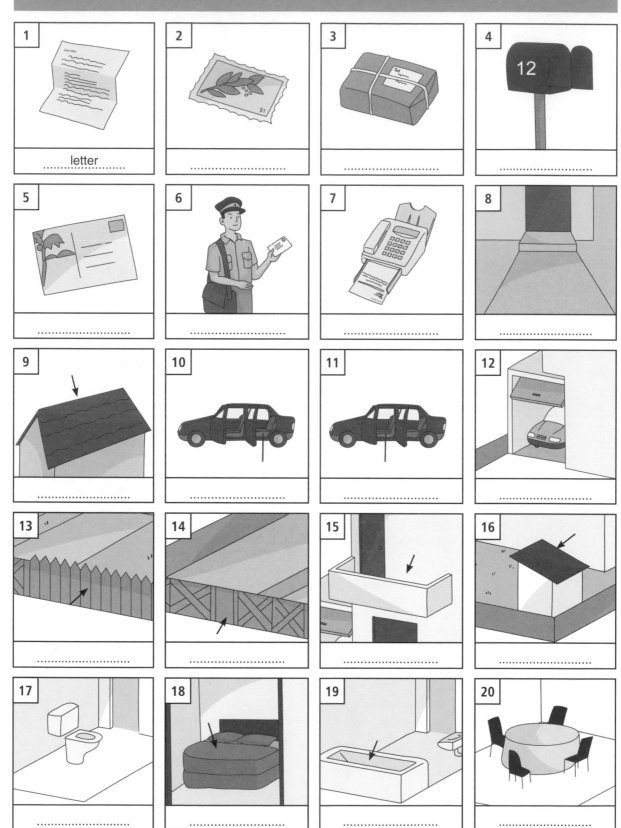

1. .... letter

2. ....

3. ....

4. ....

5. ....

6. ....

7. ....

8. ....

9. ....

10. ....

11. ....

12. ....

13. ....

14. ....

15. ....

16. ....

17. ....

18. ....

19. ....

20. ....

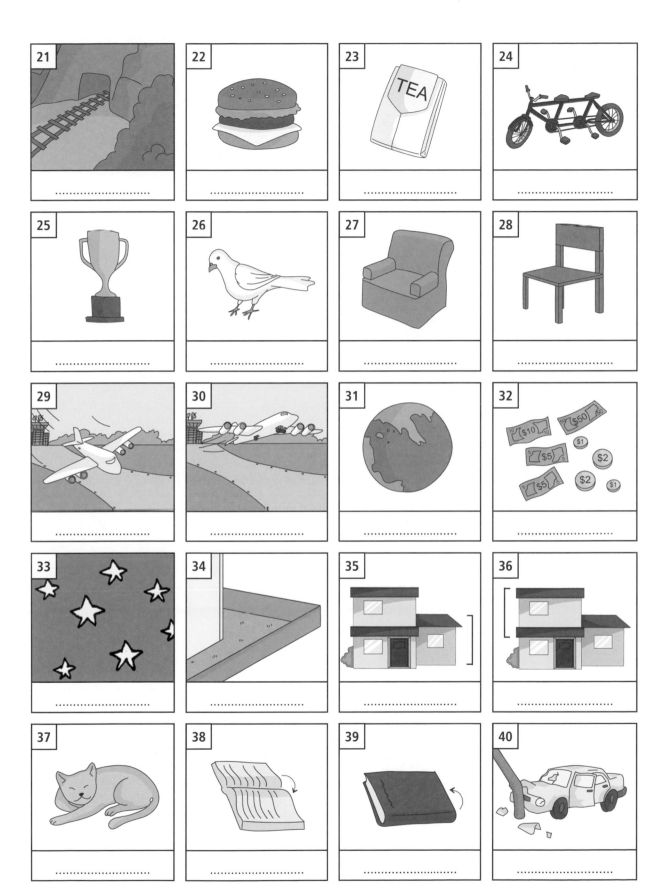

21	22	23	24
....	....	....	....
25	26	27	28
....	....	....	....
29	30	31	32
....	....	....	....
33	34	35	36
....	....	....	....
37	38	39	40
....	....	....	....

A

1. How was the flight?
2. Good to see you again.
3. I'll meet you at the airport.
4. Have you been to the art gallery?
5. This is my new car.

a. It looks great.
b. Thanks.
c. It's been a long time.
d. It was OK.
e. No, I haven't.

B

1. How have you been?
2. Where did you go last weekend?
3. Where are they going tomorrow night?
4. What are you doing tomorrow?
5. How can I help?

a. Very good.
b. I stayed at home.
c. Load the dishwasher.
d. I'm working.
e. They're going to a restaurant.

C

1. A parcel's arrived for you.
2. I'm looking forward to the flight.
3. When did the fax arrive?
4. Can we go to the movie tonight?

a. Yesterday morning.
b. Good idea.
c. Who's it from?
d. So am I.

D

1. I want to go to a restaurant.
2. This is delicious.
3. What's the best hotel around here?
4. Is this restaurant good?

a. No, and it's expensive.
b. The Grand Hotel.
c. I'd rather see a movie.
d. Thank you.

message   idea   know   How   say   another   late   happened

1

It's twenty past one.

What's happened to Jean?

2

I don't .... She said she'd be here at one.

Did she .... she'd meet us in front of the restaurant?

3

Yes.

Is there .... restaurant in the hotel?

4

Let's ask the receptionist.

Good ....

5

Excuse me. .... many restaurants are there in the hotel?

Are you Mr and Mrs Simmons?

Yes, we are.

6

Jean Trump left you this ....

She says she'll be half an hour ....

RECEPTION

47

What   are   about   to   sounds   been   another   And   time

1

Hello Brian! How have you ....?

Very good. It's good .... see you again.

2

It's been a long ....

About four years, I think.

3

How .... Jenny and the children?

Very well. We had .... child last year, a boy. What are you doing now?

4

I'm managing a shop at the airport. .... you?

I'm still working at the bank.

5

.... about bringing the family for lunch?

Thanks. Good idea.

6

How .... next Saturday?

That .... good. I'll ask Jenny.

time   before   around   bit   looking   but   at   meet   go

1 Hello, Elise speaking.

Hi Elise. It's Steven. Would you like to .... to a restaurant tonight?

2 Sounds great, ... I'm afraid I can't. I'm going to a concert with Liz.

What .... are you going?

3 The concert starts .... eight thirty.

You and Liz could have dinner .... the concert.

4 Good idea. Which restaurant?

The Rio is the best one .... here.

It's a .... expensive. I'd rather go to Big Burger.

5 OK. When can I .... you?

At six?

6 OK.

I'm .... forward to it.

49

them   from   sent   wrong   a   won't   says   flight

1

There's a fax for you.

Who's it ....?

2

FAX   Travelwise
                      Fax: 5745 7888
                      Tel: 5745 7890

To: James Wilson
Organisation: AWS
Fax: 5871 4213
From: Adam Jones

Dear James,

Your tickets for the .... to Los Angeles on 5 September arrived this morning. We will send .... to your office today.

Have a good flight!

Best regards,

Adam

3

Adam. He .... your tickets have arrived and he's sending them here.

No, that's ....

4

Adam, have you .... the tickets?

No. Is there a problem?

5

Yes. I .... be in the office again today. Can you send them to my house?

Sure.

6

Thanks.

Have .... good flight.

> you How been have

> good Very

> trip was How the

> excellent was It

> the Where's restaurant

> receptionist ask Let's the

> here best What's around restaurant the

> know don't I

> been you Have shops to the

> I No haven't

> to again It's good you see

> been It's long time a

1

➤ I can How help

➤ this you post letter Could

2

➤ want see to a movie I

➤ rather I'd go to the theatre

3

➤ go you did Where yesterday

➤ a movie went to We

4

➤ go beach Saturday Let's to next the

➤ sounds That good

5

➤ looking movie to forward the I'm

➤ am So I

6

➤ tomorrow you doing What are

➤ the art to going I'm gallery

Answers to Unit 5

Unit 5, page 44

1.	letter	5.	postcard	9.	roof	13.	fence	17.	toilet
2.	stamp	6.	postman	10.	back seat	14.	gate	18.	double bed
3.	parcel	7.	fax	11.	front seat	15.	balcony	19.	bath
4.	letterbox	8.	path	12.	garage	16.	shed	20.	dining room

Unit 5, page 45

21.	tunnel	25.	trophy	29.	land	33.	stars	37.	cat
22.	hamburger	26.	bird	30.	take off	34.	backyard	38.	open
23.	tea	27.	sofa	31.	world	35.	upstairs	39.	closed
24.	tandem	28.	chair	32.	money	36.	downstairs	40.	accident

Unit 5, page 46

A. 1d 2c 3b 4e 5a   B. 1a 2b 3e 4d 5c   C. 1c 2d 3a 4b   D. 1c 2d 3b 4a

Unit 5, page 47

1. happened   2. know, say   3. another   4. idea   5. How   6. message, late

Unit 5, page 48

1. been, to   2. time   3. are, another   4. And   5. What   6. about, sounds

Unit 5, page 49

1. go   2. but, time   3. at, before   4. around, bit   5. meet   6. looking

Unit 5, page 50

1. from   2. flight, them   3. says, wrong   4. sent   5. won't   6. a

Unit 5, page 51

1. How have you been?
   Very good.

2. How was the trip?
   It was excellent.

3. Where's the restaurant?
   Let's ask the receptionist.

4. What's the best restaurant around here?
   I don't know.

5. Have you been to the shops?
   No I haven't.

6. It's good to see you again.
   It's been a long time.

Unit 5, page 52

1. How can I help?
   Could you post this letter?

2. I want to see a movie.
   I'd rather go to the theatre.

3. Where did you go yesterday?
   We went to a movie.

4. Let's go to the beach next Saturday.
   That sounds good.

5. I'm looking forward to the movie.
   So am I.

6. What are you doing tomorrow?
   I'm going to the art gallery.

UNIT 6: You always watch movies!

In this unit you will learn the following:

- How to express hopes
- How to give preferences
- How to describe the weather

Here are the words you will learn to use:

advertisement	disappointed	kettle	remote control	switch	wet
alone	fine	light	showers	temperature	windy
channel	fish	loud	soft	thermometer	
cloudy	foggy	news	snow	together	
cold	hope	printer	sport	visit	
comedy	hot	radio	storm	weather forecast	
computer	instead	rain	sunny	weather report	

Here are some phrases you will learn to use:

turn on	turn up	I'd rather	a cloudy day	do the dishes
turn off	turn down	watch a movie	plane crash	

Here are some sentences you will practice:

Turn it up.

Tomorrow will be fine and sunny.

It's too wet to go to the park.

Can I help?

I hope it's a girl.

If we catch some fish we'll eat them for dinner.

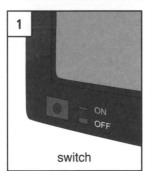

1

switch

2

The TV is on.

3

The TV is off.

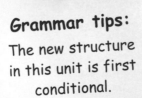

Grammar tips:
The new structure in this unit is first conditional.

4

turn the TV on

5

turn the TV off

1
a radio

2
an electric kettle

3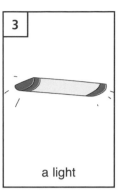
a light

4
a computer

5
a printer

6
loud

Turn it down.

Turn it up.

Turn it off.

7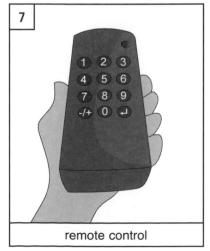
remote control

8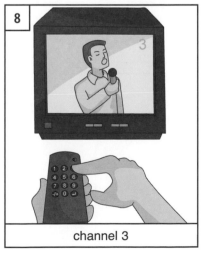
channel 3

9
channel 6

weather

**1**	**2**	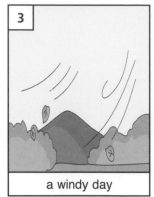**3**	**4**
a fine day, a sunny day	a cloudy day	a windy day	a rainy day, a wet day
**5**	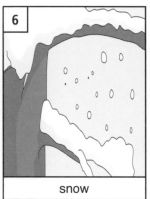**6**	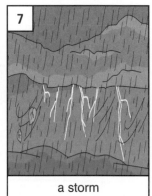**7**	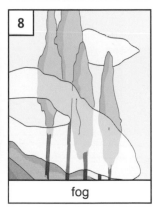**8**
showers	snow	a storm	fog

temperature

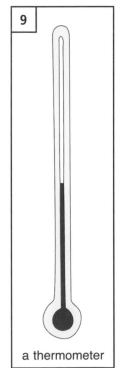

9

a thermometer

10 80 degrees — hot

11 3 degrees — cold

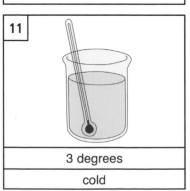

12 It was hot today with the temperature at 30 degrees.

TODAY 30°　TOMORROW 23°

a weather report

13 Tomorrow will be fine and sunny. The temperature will be 23 degrees.

TODAY 0°　TOMORROW 23°

a weather forecast

1

This morning there was a plane crash.

news

2

Victa is the best car.

an advertisement for Victa cars

3

I love you Roxanne but ...

movie

4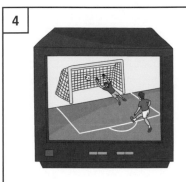

sport

5

a comedy

6

I'd like to watch the sport on channel 7.

I'd rather watch the movie on channel 8.

But you always watch movies. I never watch sport!

No, you always watch sport and I never watch movies!

Sport is more interesting. Movies are boring.

No, movies are more interesting than sport. Sport is very boring.

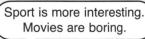 

Let's go to the park instead of watching TV.

OK.

7

It's too wet to go to the park. We'll watch this DVD instead.

57

1 alone

2 alone

3 together

4 doing the dishes alone

Can I help?

doing the dishes together

5 a visit

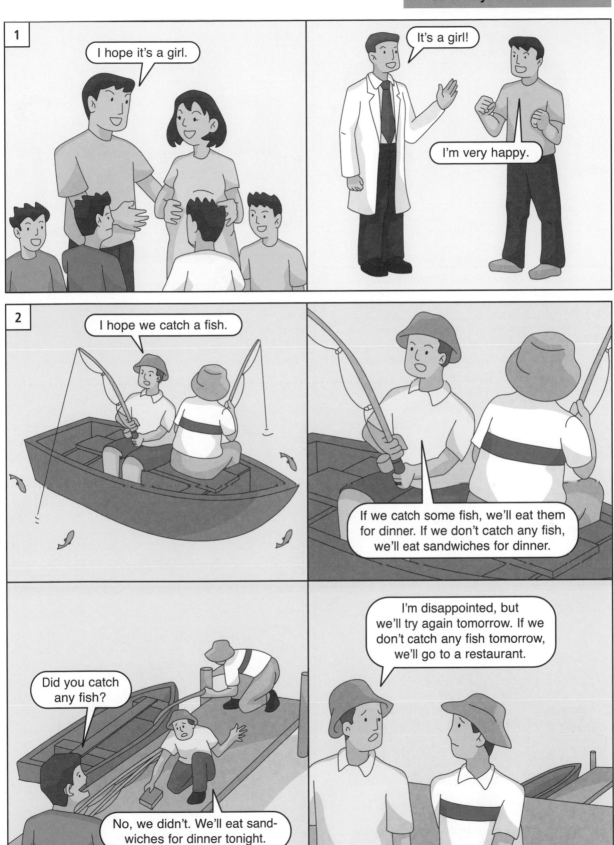

The Bensons

UNIT 7: I'd like to see a doctor.

In this unit you will learn the following:

- How to seek clarification
- How to use public transport

Here are the words you will learn to use:

attendant	exit	hair	mascara	remember	timetable	waiting room
because	express	kiosk	newsagent	return	toilets	which
busy	eyelash	lipstick	platform	single	twin	
comb	face	lost property	powder	so	umbrella	
entry	forget	luggage	ready	ticket office	via	

Here are some phrases you will learn to use:

Which one?   Go away!   Come back!   Pick up   Can you remember . . .?

Here are some sentences you will practice:

Are you ready?   I forget his name.   I'm combing my hair.

You forgot your umbrella.   Which one would you like, sir?   I'm going to the dentist.

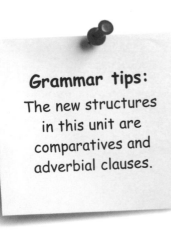

Grammar tips:
The new structures in this unit are comparatives and adverbial clauses.

A single ticket to Smithton is $5.

A return ticket to Smithton is $10.

an umbrella

1. hair
2. comb
3. lips
4. lipstick
5. eyelashes
6. mascara
7. face
8. powder

1

I can't come now. ...

... because I'm busy.

2

I can't pick up this box because it's too heavy.

It's too heavy, so he can't pick it up.

3

I can't go to the zoo tomorrow because I'm going to the dentist.

Jenny's going to the dentist tomorrow, so she can't go to the zoo.

4

Can I go out?

No, it's raining, so you can't go out.

Mum says .... because ....

5

You can't go to the park because you have to tidy your bedroom.

Mum says .... so ....

6

It's after ten o'clock now, so we have to go.

.... because ....

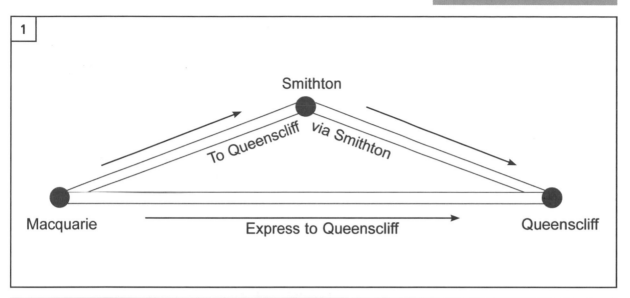

The Bensons

It's Saturday and the Benson family is getting ready to go to the zoo.

The Bensons are going to the station.

UNIT 8: Ten dollars extra.

In this unit you will learn the following:

- How to ask wh- questions
- How to say how long something takes

Here are the words you will learn to use:

antelope	finish	ice	lion	start	top	who
bottom	fur	join	operation	take	tour	why
branch	giraffe	kangaroo	pouch	tiger	what	zebra
elephant	hill	koala	seal	tree	when	
extra	how	leaf	separate	trunk	where	

Here are some phrases you will learn to use:

at the top of   at the bottom of

Here are some sentences you will practice:

The meeting starts at one o'clock.   Who's coming?   When is she coming?

The operation took five hours.   How is she coming?   Why is she coming?

When will you finish?   Where is she coming from? What will we eat?

1

finish

start

Grammar tips:
The new structures in this unit are open-ended questions and more prepositions.

2

Meeting:
1 p.m.- 2 p.m.

The meeting
takes an hour.

The meeting starts at one o'clock and finishes at two o'clock.

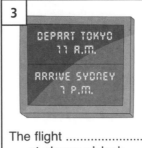

3

DEPART TOKYO
11 A.M.

ARRIVE SYDNEY
7 P.M.

The flight .... at eleven o'clock and .... at seven o'clock.

DEPART TOKYO
11 A.M.

ARRIVE SYDNEY
7 P.M.

The flight takes eight hours.

1

Monday 7 a.m.

2
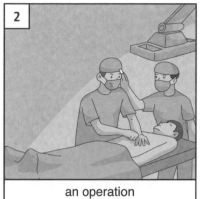
an operation

3
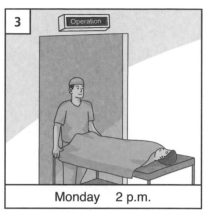
Monday 2 p.m.

4
"The operation took five hours."
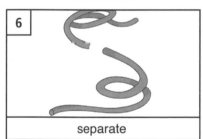
Wednesday

5
"When will you finish?"
"I don't know. It'll take a long time."
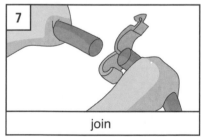

6

separate

7
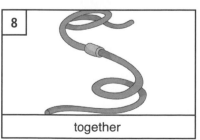
join

8

together

9
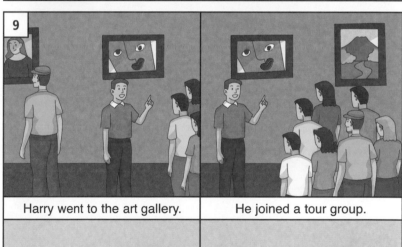
Harry went to the art gallery.

He joined a tour group.

"Where have you been, Harry?"
"I went to the art gallery."

"Did you like it?"
"Yes, I joined a tour. It was very interesting."

1

koala

branch

fur

leaf

pouch

trunk

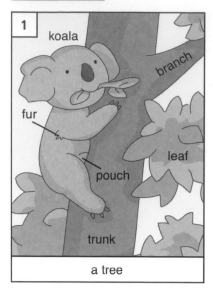

a tree

2

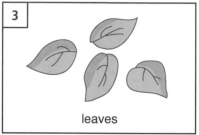

a leaf

3

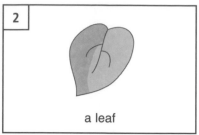

leaves

4

Koalas live in trees and eat leaves.

5

a hill

6

I live in the big house at the top of the hill.

7

I live in the small house at the bottom of the hill.

8

Write your name at the top of the page ...

... and the page number at the bottom of the page.

The Bensons

1

.... and we'd like to join a tour, please.

I'll pay.

OK, that's an extra $5 per person.

The Bensons are at the Zoo with Kim and Sue.

2

Welcome to Macquarie Zoo. My name is David, and I'm your tour guide. The tour will take about an hour. You can ask questions at any time. We'll begin by going this way, to the lions and tigers.

3

Lions are big cats. They come from Africa. They live in families.

Lions

What do they eat?

They eat other animals, like antelopes and zebras.

4

This is a giraffe. Giraffes live in Africa, too.

Why do they have long necks?

Giraffes

Because they like eating the leaves at the tops of the trees.

5

Who knows what this is?

I know. It's a koala.

That's right. Koalas live in Australia and they eat leaves, too. They live in the trees.

Where do they sleep?

They sleep in the trees, too.

UNIT 9: Where is Sue?

In this unit you will learn the following:

- How to give a location
- How to express possibility

Here are the words you will learn to use:

around	closed	further	maybe	possibly	sit	wardrobe
behind	crawl	horse	might	probably	stand	
beside	far	hotel lobby	on	race	under	
boxer	fight	jockey	open	room service	vending machine	
close	fly	lie	over	run	walk	

Here are some phrases you will learn to use:

too loud   not big enough   in front of

Here are some sentences you will practice:

He might jump over it.   Maybe the restaurant is still open.

Where's my pen?   There's probably a restaurant open

Tony's sitting on it.   around here somewhere.

Grammar tips:

The new structures in this unit are adverbs of probability and more prepositions.

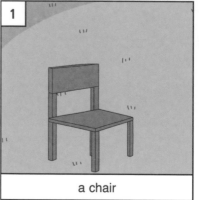

1

a chair

2

Tony's sitting on it.

3

Wilma's standing beside it.

4

Bob's walking behind it.

5

Paul's running around it.

6

A bird's flying over it.

A baby's crawling under it.

A dog's lying in front of it.

John's taking a picture of it.

I want to take a picture of that. Where's my camera?

On the table.

Where's the cat?

Under the table.

Where's the dog?

.... the sofa.

Where's Jim?

.... his house.

Where's my umbrella?

.... the TV.

.... the bed.

Where are my shoes?

Where's my pen?

.... the table.

1

a horse

2

a jockey

3

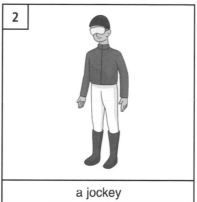

a horse race

4

Will number 7 win? ....

5

Will number 13 win? ....

6

Will number 4 win? ....

7

a boxer

8

a fight

9

10

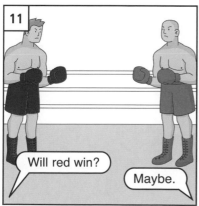

11

12

13

1

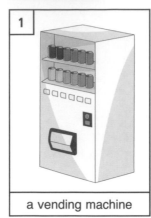

a vending machine

2

a hotel lobby

3

room service

4

reception

5

I'd like something to eat.

Maybe the restaurant is still open. I'll ask at reception.

6

Is the restaurant still open?

I'm sorry sir, the restaurant is closed now.

7

You can get a room service and there's a vending machine in the hotel lobby.

Thank you.

8

Let's go out. There's probably a restaurant open around here somewhere.

Yes, good idea.

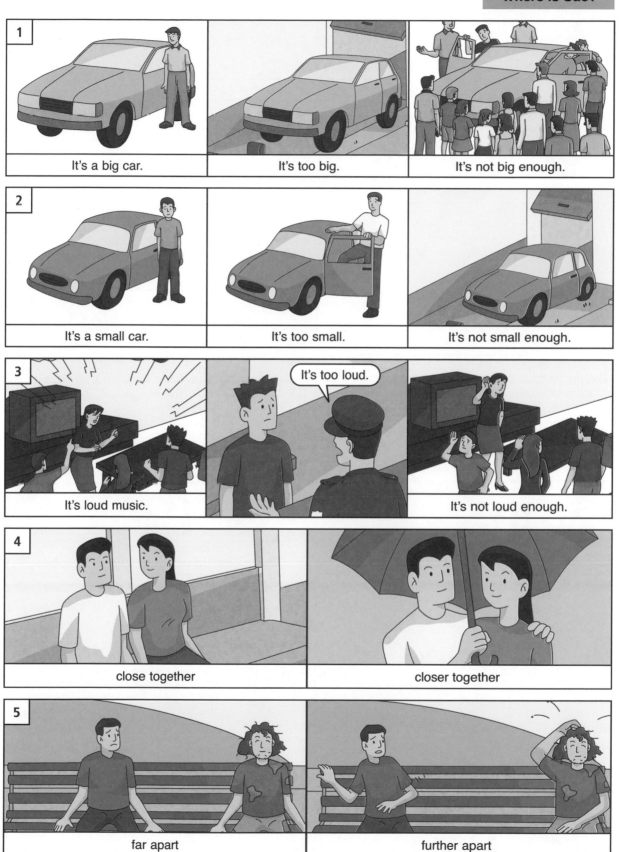

1. It's a big car. | It's too big. | It's not big enough.

2. It's a small car. | It's too small. | It's not small enough.

3. It's loud music. | It's too loud. | It's not loud enough.

4. close together | closer together

5. far apart | further apart

The Bensons

The Bensons are at the zoo.
Tom is taking a picture in front of the koalas.

UNIT 10: Revision and extension

1 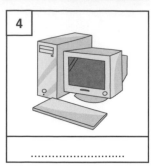 ....radio.........	**2**	**3** 	**4** 
5 	**6** 	**7** 	**8** 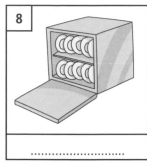
9 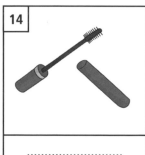	**10** 	**11** 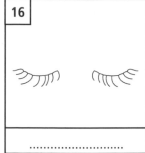	**12** 
13 	**14** 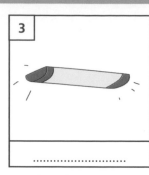	**15** 	**16**
17 	**18** 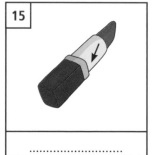	**19**	**20**

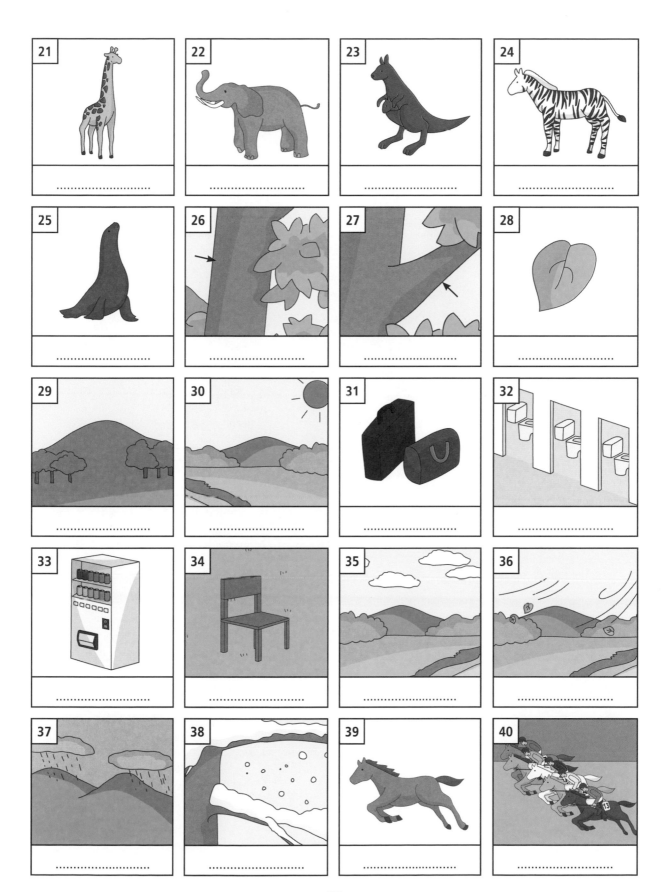

A

1. I'd rather watch TV than go swimming.
2. Can I help with the dishes?
3. Have you got your suitcase?
4. Are you ready to go?
5. Two to the airport, please.

a. Single or return?
b. Almost.
c. So would I.
d. Yes, I have.
e. No, it's all right.

B

1. Where's the camera?
2. I never watch TV.
3. Why did you buy a new house?
4. What time are we leaving?
5. Where are the toilets?

a. At a quarter past two.
b. I've got it.
c. Beside the entrance.
d. I didn't know that.
e. Because we needed more bedrooms.

C

1. Do you watch sport on TV?
2. When does the news start?
3. The radio's too loud.
4. Can you turn the TV off ?
5. Where are the tickets?

a. I'll turn it down.
b. I forgot them.
c. Six o'clock.
d. Sometimes.
e. Sure.

D

1. What channel's the movie on?
2. Can you turn the printer off?
3. We'd like to join a tour.
4. When does the tour finish?
5. Which video would you like?

a. At one thirty.
b. This one.
c. That'll be twelve dollars each.
d. Channel seven.
e. Where's the switch?

in	channel	open	about	where	beside	on

1

The tv and fridge are in here. You can get movies on channel 3.

OK, and where can I put my luggage?

2

Your suitcases can go .... the wardrobe. The bathroom is through there.

Good. What .... the phone?

3

The phone's .... that table. Ring nine for reception and three first for other calls.

Is there a fax?

4

Yes. It's .... there.

OK, and when does the restaurant .... for dinner?

5

At six o'clock.

Thank you.

Enjoy your stay.

without   might   rather   instead   down   enough   like   so

1 Can I help you?

Yes. I'd .... a large suitcase but it must be light.

2 Is that one big ....?

It's too big.

3 What about that one?

Yes. That looks OK. Could you get it .... for me?

Of course.

4 It's light enough, but I'd .... have one with wheels.

We .... have one. I'll check.

5 This one's for planes, ... it's very light and has wheels.

It looks OK.

6 It's light enough. How much is it?

$295.

7 Oh! How much was the one .... wheels?

$169

8 I'll take it ....

does	take	open	extra	start	from	tours	before

1

The Jameson Art Gallery. Colin speaking.

Good morning. When is the gallery ....?

2

The gallery's open .... nine a.m. to four thirty from Monday to Saturday. It's closed on Sundays.

Thanks. And how much .... it cost?

3

Seven dollars.

Do you have ....?

4

They're an .... three dollars.

When do they .... and how long do they take?

5

There are two tours. They .... two hours and start at nine thirty and one thirty. You need to arrive about fifteen minutes .... the start.

6

Thanks.

get   When   arriving   finish   Where   Why

1 .... are we going today?

The zoo and then the park.

2 .... are we going to the park?

We're having lunch there.

3 How long does it take to .... to the zoo?

She said it takes half an hour.

4 .... do we get to the park?

At one o'clock.

Thanks.

5 When does the tour ....?

At four o'clock.

Thanks.

6 We're now .... at the zoo.

1

Do you want to watch tv?

I'd rather read a book.

➤ want watch to TV you Do
➤ rather I'd a book read

2

......................?

....

➤ wallet Where's my
➤ forgot Maybe it you

3

....

....

➤ to city Three the please
➤ two each dollars That's

4

......................?

....

➤ is Where telephone the
➤ reception Beside

5

....

....

➤ I watching sport like
➤ So I do

6

......................?

....

➤ start does When the movie
➤ news the After

93

1

➤ late you Why are

➤ wrong went the restaurant I to

2

➤ buy suitcase we Can a new

➤ enough we got Have money

3

➤ taxi get Where I a can

➤ hotel the of front In

4

➤ a tour join like to I'd

➤ tour next starts The nine o'clock at

5

➤ would see you like movie Which to

➤ one This

6

➤ video do that Why you want

➤ It be might interesting.

Answers to Unit 10

Unit 10, page 86

1. radio	5. printer	9. kiosk	13. comb	17. box
2. kettle	6. CD player	10. timetable	14. mascara	18. lion
3. light	7. video	11. thermometer	15. lipstick	19. tiger
4. computer	8. dishwasher	12. umbrella	16. eyelashes	20. koala

Unit 10, page 87

21. giraffe	25. seal	29. hill	33. vending machine	37. rain
22. elephant	26. trunk	30. sunny	34. chair	38. snow
23. kangaroo	27. branch	31. luggage	35. cloudy	39. horse
24. zebra	28. leaf	32. toilets	36. windy	40. horse race

Unit 10, page 88

A. 1c 2e 3d 4b 5a   B. 1b 2d 3e 4a 5c   C. 1d 2c 3a 4e 5b   D. 1d 2e 3c 4a 5b

Unit 10, page 89

1. channel, where   2. beside, about   3. on   4. in, open

Unit 10, page 90

1. like   2. enough   3. down   4. rather, might   5. so   7. without   8 instead

Unit 10, page 92

1. open   2. from, does   3. tours   4. extra, start   5. take, before

Unit 5, page 50

1. Where   2. Why   3. get   4. When   5. finish   6. arriving

Unit 10, page 93

1. Do you want to watch TV?
   I'd rather read a book.

2. Where's my wallet?
   Maybe you forgot it.

3. Three to the city please.
   That's two dollars each.

4. Where is the telephone?
   Beside reception.

5. I like watching sport.
   So do I.

6. When does the movie start?
   After the news.

Unit 10, page 94

1. Why are you late?
   I went to the wrong restaurant.

2. Can we buy a new suitcase?
   Have we got enough money?

3. Where can I get a taxi?
   In front of the hotel.

4. I'd like to join a tour.
   The next tour starts at nine o'clock.

5. Which movie would you like to see?
   This one.

6. Why do you want that video?
   It might be interesting.

UNIT 11: I'm wearing one, too.

In this unit you will learn the following:

- How to talk about clothes
- How to say what's wrong with something

Here are the words you will learn to use:

bottom drawer	creased	hat	jumper	skirt	tie	work
bra	dirty	herself	mark	socks	top drawer	worried
burnt	dress	himself	myself	stockings	torn	yourself
chest of drawers	dresser	hole	ourselves	suit	trousers	yourselves
clean	either	jacket	pants	themselves	wardrobe	
coat	fall	jeans	shirt	tee shirt	wear	

Here are some phrases you will learn to use:

might be   must be   in case   doesn't work

Here are some sentences you will practice:

She's dressing herself.

Did you hurt yourself?

That must be Mr Ross.

There's a hole in it.

I'm not wearing any either.

I'm wearing a hat.

Grammar tips:

The new structures in this unit are reflexive pronouns, modals of deduction and adverbs of agreement.

1

Come here Anna, and I'll dress you.

Where's Mum?

She's dressing Anna.

1992

Anna, go and dress yourself.

1996

2

Where's Anna?

She's in her bedroom. She's dressing herself.

Anna, where are you?

I'm in my bedroom. I'm dressing myself.

3

We're dressing ourselves.

They're dressing themselves.

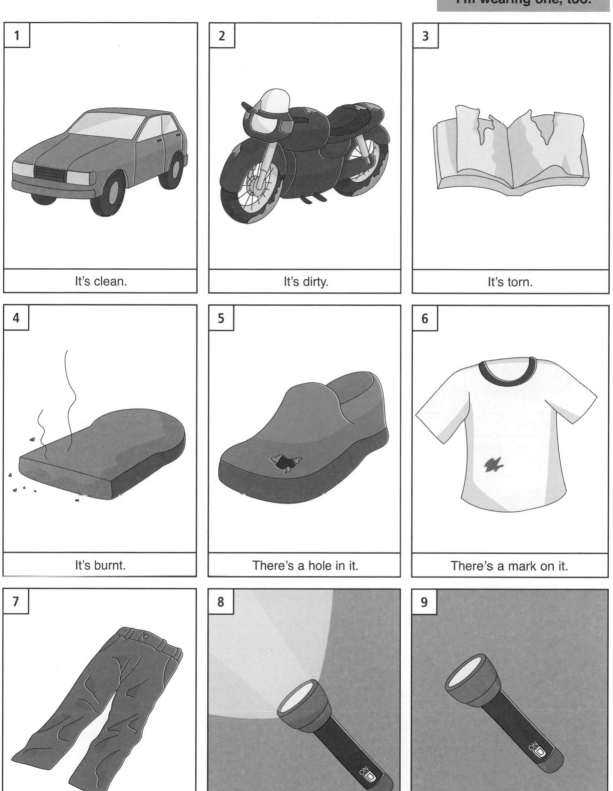

1 It's clean.	**2** It's dirty.	**3** It's torn.
4 It's burnt.	**5** There's a hole in it.	**6** There's a mark on it.
7 They're creased.	**8** It works.	**9** It doesn't work.

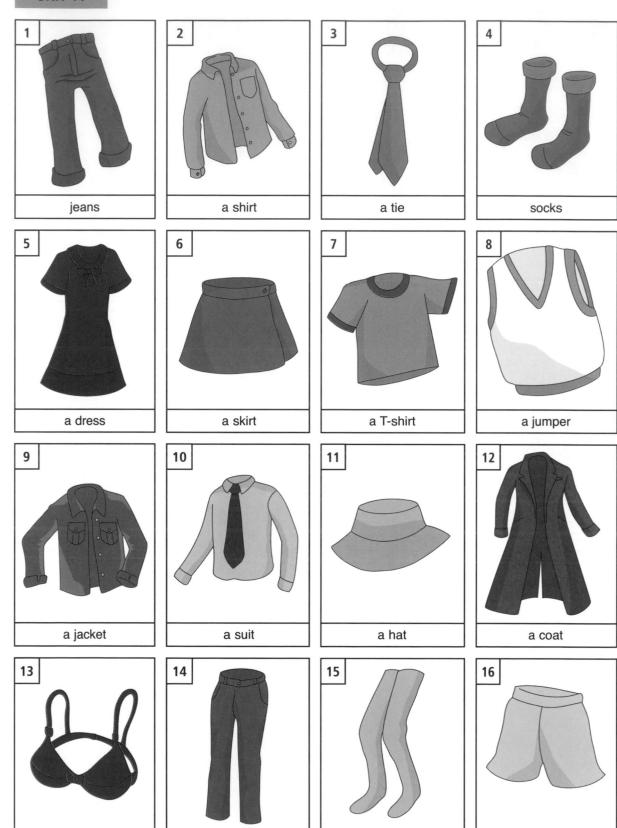

1 jeans	**2** a shirt
3 a tie	**4** socks
5 a dress	**6** a skirt
7 a T-shirt	**8** a jumper
9 a jacket	**10** a suit
11 a hat	**12** a coat
13 a bra	**14** trousers
15 stockings	**16** pants

1

a wardrobe

2

Where's your suit?

In the wardrobe.

3

a dresser

4

Where are your jeans?

On the dresser.

5

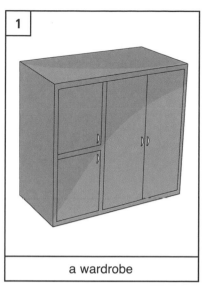

a chest of drawers

6

Where is your T-shirt?

In the top drawer.

7

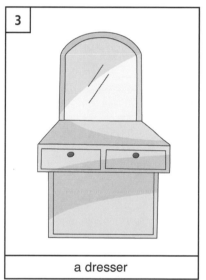

Where are your socks?

In the bottom drawer.

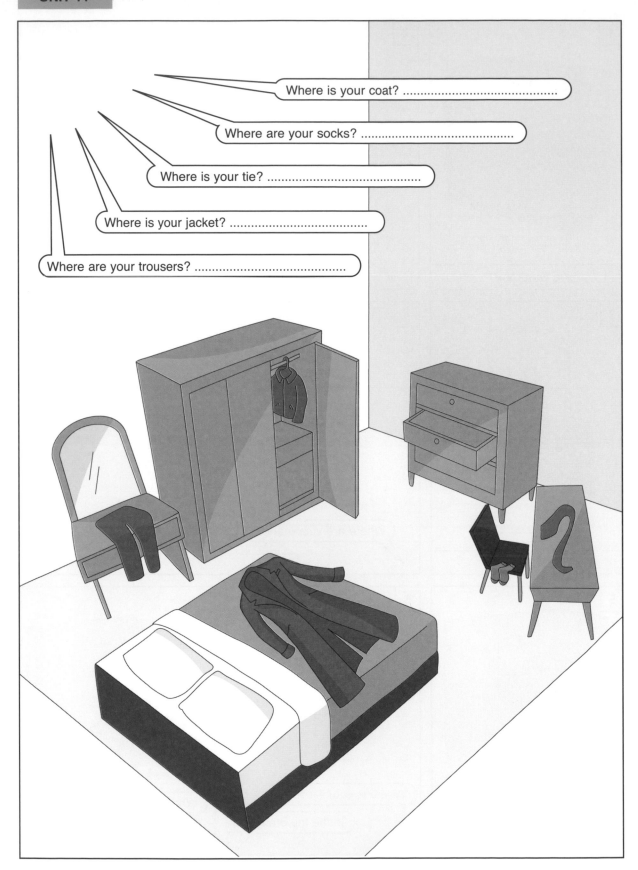

1

I'm wearing a hat.

2

I'm wearing one too.

3

I'm not wearing a hat.

4

I'm not wearing one either.

5

I'm wearing shoes.

6

I'm wearing some too.

7

I'm not wearing shoes.

8

I'm not wearing any either.

The Bensons

105

UNIT 12: You'd better go to the dentist.

In this unit you will learn the following:

- How to give advice
- How to compare things with each other

Here are the words you will learn to use:

bench	happy	room	unhappy
comfortable	hurry	safe	unpack
dentist	motorbike	truck	unsafe
done up	move	uncomfortable	x-ray
fix	pack	undone	

Here are some phrases you will learn to use:

you'd better   you should   good idea   have it . . . -ed

Grammar tips:
The new structures in this unit are causatives, comparatives and adjectives with un- .

Here are some sentences you will practice:

I've got a toothache.   I'll have it fixed.

You'd better take an umbrella.   Can you move your arm?

We'd better have it checked?   A truck is safer than a motorbike.

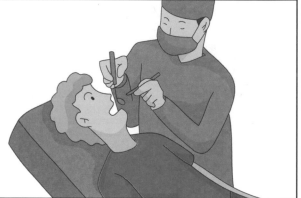

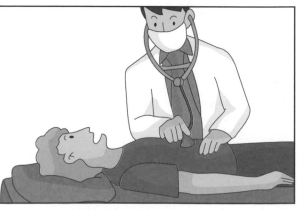

1. happy
2. unhappy
3. comfortable
4. uncomfortable
5. done up
6. undone
7. packed
8. unpacked
9. safe
10. unsafe

11.

He's too big. There's not enough room for him.

Now there is enough room for me.

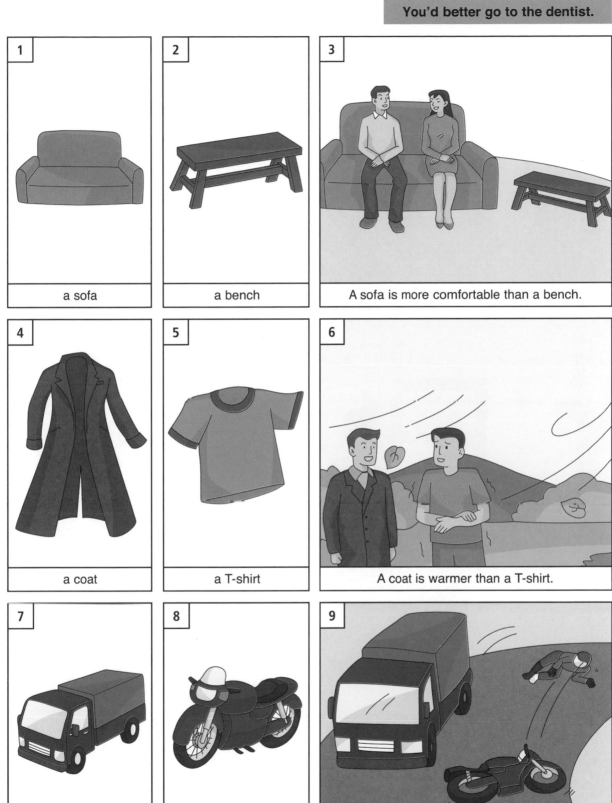

1   a sofa

2   a bench

3   A sofa is more comfortable than a bench.

4   a coat

5   a T-shirt

6   A coat is warmer than a T-shirt.

7   a truck

8   a motorbike

9   A truck is safer than a motorbike.

The Bensons

UNIT 13: I was having breakfast when the phone rang.

In this unit you will learn the following:
- How to describe medical problems
- How to make recommendations
- How to describe interrupted events

Here are the words you will learn to use:

arm	bruised	cough	eye	knee	rash	swollen
band aid	careful	crutches	few	medicine	rest	tablet
bandage	careless	cut	finger	mouth	scratch	thumb
birthday	caution	danger	hair	nose	show	tongue
bite	chest	exercise	itchy	prescription	soon	until

Here are some phrases you will learn to use:

take off   put on   stay in bed   stop smoking

Here are some sentences you will practice:

You should take off your jacket.   You should stop smoking.

I was having breakfast when   Show him your ticket.
    the phone rang.   I burnt my arm.

You need more exercise.   You can't go until your bedroom is tidy.

Grammar tips:
The new structures in this unit are modals of obligation and interrupted past.

1 I was having breakfast when the phone rang.

2 It was my mother. I was talking to her when the doorbell rang.

3 It was my father. I was talking to my father at the front door when the post-man came and gave me a letter.

4 It was from my brother. I was reading the letter from my brother when my mobile phone rang.

5 It was my sister.

6 They all said "Happy birthday!"

114

1

What's the problem?

I've got an earache.

2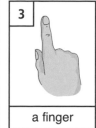
a tongue

3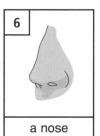
a finger

4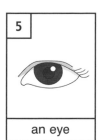
a thumb

5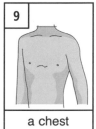
an eye

6
a nose

7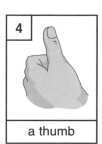
a mouth

8
hair

9
a chest

10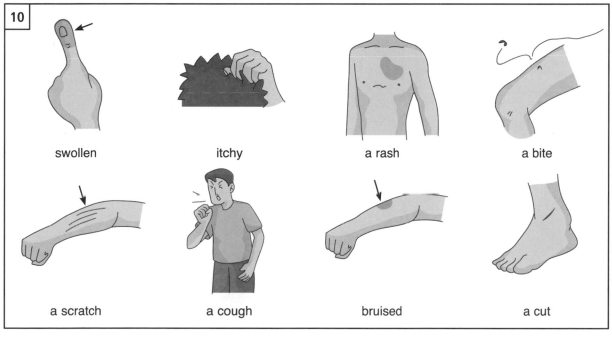

swollen   itchy   a rash   a bite

a scratch   a cough   bruised   a cut

11
I've got a rash on my arm.

12
My head's itchy.

13
My thumb's swollen.

14
I cut my finger.

115

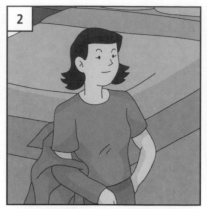

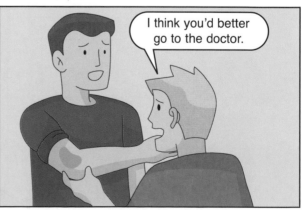

1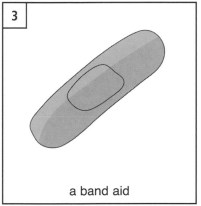

Show me your tongue.

2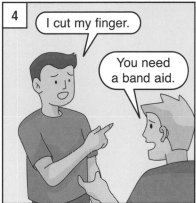

Show him your ticket.

3

a band aid

4

I cut my finger.

You need a band aid.

5

6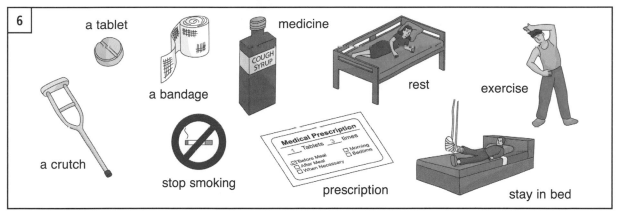

a tablet

a bandage

medicine

rest

exercise

a crutch

stop smoking

prescription

stay in bed

7

You should stop smoking.

8

You need more exercise.

117

I was having breakfast when the phone rang.

careful

careless

119

The Bensons

1 How can I help you? — I fell and hurt my leg.

Sue has fallen at the zoo and hurt her leg.
She is at the hospital.

2 Tell me how it happened. — I was at the zoo with my family when I fell.

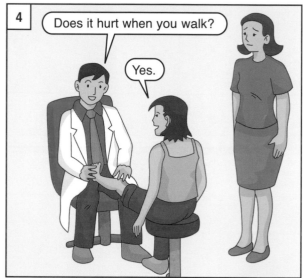

3 I'd better have a look at it. Show me where it hurts. — Here.

4 Does it hurt when you walk? — Yes.

5 Does it hurt here? — Yes, it does.

6 It's swollen and bruised but I don't think it's broken. I'll put a bandage on it and you'd better rest for a few days.

UNIT 14: Do you have a receipt?

In this unit you will learn the following:

- How to buy or rent things
- How to talk about size
- How to talk about distance

Here are the words you will learn to use:

battery	distance	handbag	lights	plus	sign
borrow	drill	height	long	point	signature
car rental firm	driver's licence	high	limit	receipt	unlimited
centimetre	equals	include	metre	refund	wheel
cheque	exchange	insurance (company)	minus	registration number	wide
damage	far	kilometre	mirror	rent	width
deposit	form	lend	panel beater	saw	windsurfer
discount	hammer	length	percent	scarf	

Here are some phrases you will learn to use:

for sale   total price   divided by   multiplied by   I'm afraid   fill out

Here are some sentences you will practice:

Can I borrow your saw, please?   You need a ten percent deposit.   How far is Meltone?

Could I have a receipt, please?   Eight divided by four equals two.

Can I have a refund, please?   Does that include ten percent discount?

 a saw

Can I borrow your saw, please?
OK.

Thank you.

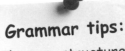

Grammar tips:
The new structures in this unit are mathematical relationships and prediction with 'will'.

Alan was sawing some wood when his saw broke. He went next door to borrow Jeff's saw. Jeff agreed and gave Alan the saw. Alan finished sawing the wood and brought the saw back to Jeff.

1

a drill   a hammer   a handbag   a scarf

2

Can I borrow your hammer, please?

3

Would you lend me your handbag, please?

4

Would you .... your scarf, please?

5

I'd like to .... $80,000, please.

6

$27,000 $25,000 $33,000

CARS FOR SALE

7

$80 a day $95 a day

CARS FOR RENT

8

$110 a day

I'll have to rent a car, because I don't have enough money to buy one.

CARS FOR RENT

9

$80 a day

He said he .... , so ....

CARS FOR RENT

+	**-**	**X**	**÷**	**=**	**%**	**.**
plus	minus	multiplied by	divided by	equals	percent	point

2 Eight plus four equals twelve.

$$8 + 4 = 12$$

3 Eight minus four equals four.

$$8 - 4 = 4$$

4 Eight multiplied by four equals thirty-two.

$$8 \times 4 = 32$$

5 Eight divided by four equals two.

$$8 \div 4 = 2$$

6 Fifty percent of eight equals four.

$$50\% \text{ of } 8 = 4$$

7 Twenty five percent of ten equals two point five.

$$25\% \text{ of } 10 = 2.5$$

8

a battery

9

$8 includes batteries

Total price $8

10

$1 each $7 batteries not included

Total price $9

11

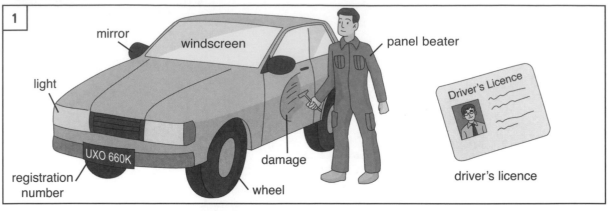

John Smith is signing his name.

a signature

a form

filling out a form

signing a form

1

Last year I had an accident.

2

I rang the insurance company.

3

I filled out a form.

4

The insurance company gave me $7000.

5

I used the money to have the car fixed.

6

Now my car is fixed and I'm happy.

1

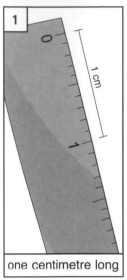

one centimetre long

2

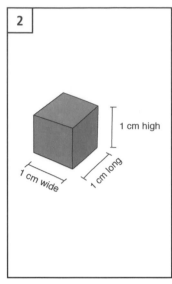

1 cm high
1 cm wide
1 cm long

3

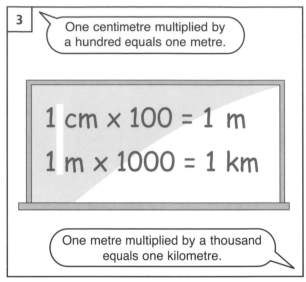

One centimetre multiplied by a hundred equals one metre.

$$1 \text{ cm} \times 100 = 1 \text{ m}$$
$$1 \text{ m} \times 1000 = 1 \text{ km}$$

One metre multiplied by a thousand equals one kilometre.

4

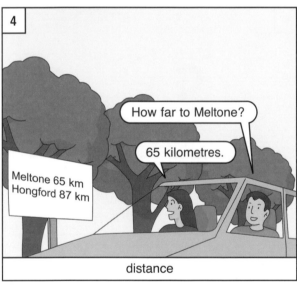

How far to Meltone?

65 kilometres.

Meltone 65 km
Hongford 87 km

distance

5

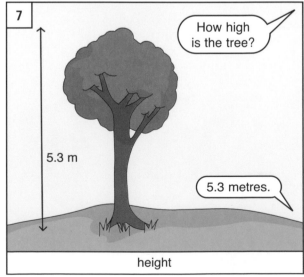

2 metres.

Windsurfer $299

How long is the windsurfer?

length

6

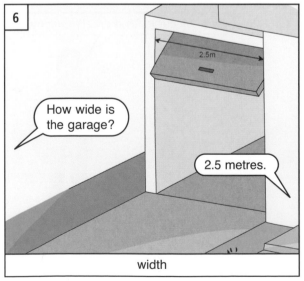

2.5m

How wide is the garage?

2.5 metres.

width

7

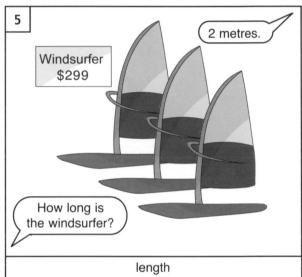

How high is the tree?

5.3 m

5.3 metres.

height

128

The Bensons

7 Yes, that one is $65 a day. I'll check to see if we have one.

8 I'm sorry, sir. I'm afraid they're all out this week. How about a Sonar? It's only $5 a day extra.

Yes, that's fine. Does the price include insurance and unlimited kilometres?

9 No, insurance is not included.

It's $13 a day extra and it's 10 cents a kilometre over two hundred kilometres a day, but there is a ten percent discount if you rent the car for a week.

10 Can I get one today?

Yes, and I almost forgot that there's a deposit of $750 in case you damage the car. You can use your credit card for that. Can I see your driver's licence, please?

Yes, of course.

11 Would you sign here, please?

12 Here are the keys.

Which car is it?

13 The registration number is LUG 303.

Thank you.

UNIT 15: Revision and extension

1
wardrobe

2
....

3
....

4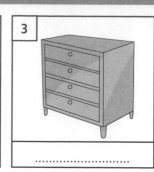
....

5
....

6
....

7
....

8
....

9
....

10
....

11
....

12
....

13
....

14
....

15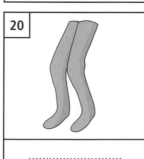
....

16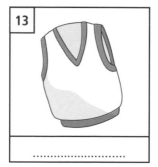
....

17
....

18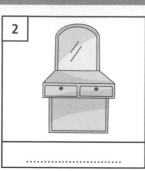
....

19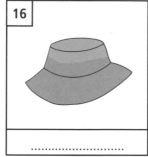
....

20
....

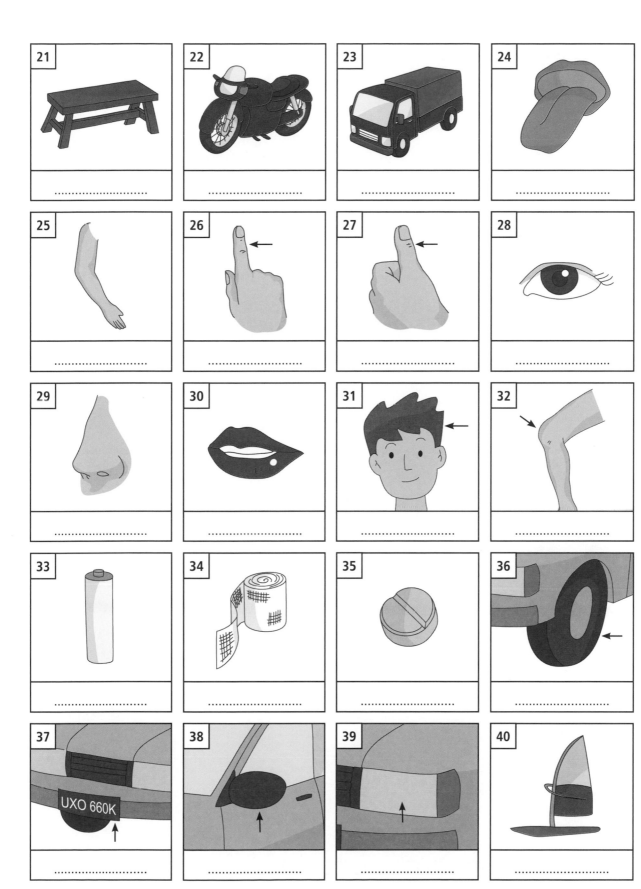

21 ....

22 ....

23 ....

24 ....

25 ....

26 ....

27 ....

28 ....

29 ....

30 ....

31 ....

32 ....

33 ....

34 ....

35 ....

36 ....

37 UXO 660K ....

38 ....

39 ....

40 ....

A

1. What's the matter?
2. Does it hurt?
3. Where's my T-shirt?
4. We'd better go home.
5. My watch is broken.

a. You'd better have it fixed.
b. Good idea.
c. Yes, it does.
d. In the top drawer.
e. I hurt myself.

B

1. What's the problem?
2. I've got a bad cough.
3. Will the bus come soon?
4. There's a mark on my new shirt.
5. Sign here please.

a. You should get a refund.
b. OK.
c. You should stop smoking.
d. My finger's swollen.
e. In a few minutes.

C

1. I've burnt my hand.
2. I'm very tired.
3. I've got a toothache.
4. Does that include a discount?
5. Where's the umbrella?

a. It might be in the car.
b. Yes, 10%.
c. You might need a bandage.
d. You'd better go to the dentist.
e. You need to rest.

D

1. My hand's swollen.
2. I'm cold.
3. Can I borrow your pen?
4. This chair's uncomfortable.
5. Do you need a deposit?

a. Sure.
b. You'd better get another one.
c. You'd better see a doctor.
d. Yes, 10%.
e. You should put on a jumper.

show	you	to	better	refund	on

1

There's a mark on this shirt. I'm getting a refund.

You'd .... take your receipt in case you have to show it.

2

Excuse me.

Yes, can I help you?

3

I hope so. I bought this shirt here this morning and there's a mark on it.

Can you .... me?

4

Would you like .... exchange it?

I'd rather have a ....

5

OK. Have .... got your receipt?

Yes. Here.

6

So that's thirty nine dollars.

Thank you.

too   before   your   rather   deposit   one

1

This one looks good.

TO RENT

I'd .... have this one.

2

Can I help you?

We'd like to rent this one.

TO RENT

No, this one.

3

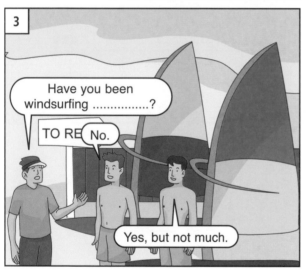

Have you been windsurfing ....?

TO RE... No.

Yes, but not much.

4

Then that one's too long and much .... heavy. You should take the smaller .... but you'd better be careful.

TO RENT

OK. How much is it?

5

Twenty dollars per hour and a refundable .... of a hundred dollars.

OK.

6

And I'll need .... name, address and signature here.

TO RENT

Sure.

| it | the | doesn't | to | new | If | there's | few | at | when |

1
The camera doesn't work.

It might need a .... battery.

2
No. I bought a new one last week.

It must be broken. We'd better have it fixed soon. I want to use it .... we go to the park on Saturday.

3
I'll take it .... the camera shop tomorrow morning.

OK.

4
Can you check this camera? I think .... something wrong with it.

What's .... problem?

5
This button .... work.

I see. We should be able to fix that.

6
How long will .... take?

A .... hours. Would three o'clock be OK?

7
Yes. .... it's going to cost more than fifty dollars, can you phone me?

Sure. Can I have your number?

It's 7751 6800.

8
Thanks. I'll see you .... three.

should	borrow	know

1

Oh no!

2

I'm sorry. I don't .... how it happened.

Let's check the damage.

3

There's a small dent here and my light's broken.

There's not much damage but we .... tell our insurance companies.

4

So we need registration numbers, names and addresses, telephone numbers and insurance companies.

OK. Can I .... a pen?

Sure.

5

6

Thanks.

OK.

1

These trousers are torn.

You should get a refund.

➤ trousers These torn are

➤ a get You refund should

2

➤ dishwasher doesn't The work

➤ better it have fixed We'd

3

....?

➤ laptop you bring did your Why

➤ case In some do work I

4

....?

....................................?

➤ I Can a this refund for get shirt

➤ got Have receipt a you

5

➤ headache a got I've

➤ too got I've one

6

➤ walked kilometres ten We've

➤ tired be must You

➤ doesn't telephone This work

➤ work either one doesn't This

➤ are too trousers These small new

➤ better them exchange You'd

➤ my phone Where's mobile

➤ in It the might kitchen be

➤ I my find can't licence driver's

➤ It here must be around somewhere

➤ matter What's the

➤ a on got my rash arm I've

➤ When the start does movie

➤ few In minutes a

Answers to Unit 15

Unit 15, page 132

1. wardrobe
2. dresser
3. chest of drawers
4. top drawer
5. bottom drawer
6. shirt
7. jeans
8. tie
9. socks
10. dress
11. skirt
12. T-shirt
13. jumper
14. coat
15. suit
16. hat
17. pants
18. bra
19. trousers
20. stockings

Unit 15, page 133

21. bench
22. motorbike
23. truck
24. tongue
25. arm
26. finger
27. thumb
28. eye
29. nose
30. mouth
31. hair
32. knee
33. battery
34. bandage
35. tablet
36. wheel
37. registration number
38. mirror
39. lights
40. windsurfer

Unit 15, page 134

A. 1e 2c 3d 4b 5a   B. 1d 2c 3e 4a 5b   C. 1c 2e 3d 4b 5a   D. 1c 2e 3a 4b 5d

Unit 15, page 135

1. on, better   3. show   4. to, refund   5. you

Unit 15, page 136

1. rather   3. before   4. too, one   5. deposit   6. your

Unit 15, page 137

1. new   2. when   3. to   4. there's, the   5. doesn't   6. it, few   7. If   8. at

Unit 15, page 138

2. know   3. should   4. borrow

Unit 15, page 139

1. These trousers are torn.
   You should get a refund.

2. The dishwasher doesn't work.
   We'd better have it fixed.

3. Why did you bring your laptop?
   In case I do some work.

4. Can I get a refund for this shirt?
   Have you got a receipt?

5. I've got a headache.
   I've got one too.

6. We've walked ten kilometres.
   You must be tired.

Unit 15, page 140

1. This telephone doesn't work.
   This one doesn't work either.

2. These new trousers are too small.
   You'd better exchange them.

3. Where's my mobile phone?
   It might be in the kitchen.

4. I can't find my driver's licence.
   It must be around here somewhere.

5. What's the matter?
   I've got a rash on my arm.

6. When does the movie start?
   In a few minutes.

UNIT 16: Can I try them on?

In this unit you will learn the following:

- What to say when you are shopping
- How to talk about consequences

Here are the words you will learn to use:

other	price	sale	same	size	special

Here are some phrases you will learn to use:

half price	anything else	just right	other one	over there	try on	pair of

Here are some sentences you will practice:

They are the same price.

They're only half price.

They're just right.

It's too much.

The big one is more expensive than the small one.

Would you like anything else?

Can I try them on?

1 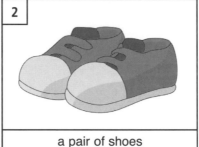 a shoe	**2** 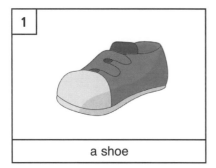 a pair of shoes
3  the size	**4** 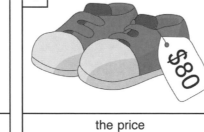 the price
5  10% off	**6** 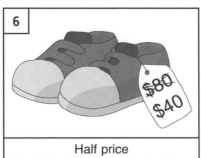 Half price

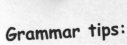

Grammar tips:

The new structure in this unit is more about comparatives.

1

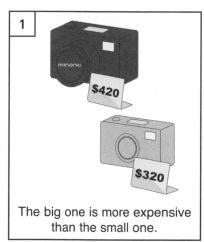

The big one is more expensive than the small one.

2

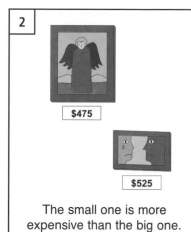

The small one is more expensive than the big one.

3

They are the same price.

4

Look. They're having a sale. Everything is cheap.

5

Look. They're on special. They're only half price.

6

Can I try them on?

Yes, of course.

They're too small.

7

Can I try them on?

Yes, of course.

You can try them on over there.

The Bensons

1

I need a new pair of jeans and a T-shirt. Would you like to come and help me buy them, Aunt Peggy? Anne is coming too.

I'd love to.

Sue tore her jeans when she fell at the zoo.

2

Sale

20% Off

10% Off

Half Price

Look, Sue. This shop is having a sale. Let's see what they have.

OK

3

I like these. Do you think they'll fit? They're size ten.

Maybe you can try them on.

4

Can I help you?

Yes. I like these jeans. Can I try them on?

Of course.

5

They're too long.

Yes, but they look good. They might have a shorter pair.

6

Do you have a shorter pair in the same size?

I'll check.

UNIT 17: Neither can I.

In this unit you will learn the following:

- How to talk about meals and food

Here are the words you will learn to use:

bean	cow	fish	order	rice	terrible
beef	delicious	hungry	peas	serve	thirsty
bowl	dessert	lamb	pig	service	tomato
bunch	entrée	main course	plate	sheep	until
cabbage	everyone	menu	pork	so	vegetable
carrot	everything	neither	potato	soup	
cauliflower	everywhere	onion	recommend	swim	

Here are some phrases you will learn to use:

a plate of . . .   a bowl of . . .   a bunch of . . .

Here are some sentences you will practice:

I'd like to book a table for four at 7:30, please.   I'll have fish.
We didn't have dessert until 11 o'clock.   She can swim.
The service was very slow.   I don't like onions.
Put everything in the suitcase.

Grammar tips:

The new structure in this unit is modals of ability.

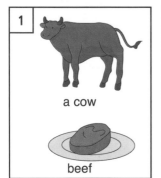

a cow

beef

a sheep

lamb

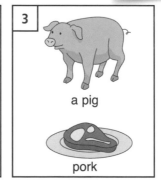

a pig

pork

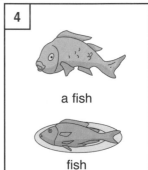

a fish

fish

I'll have fish.

So will I.

1  a plate of rice	**2**  I'm having rice.	**3**  So am I.
4 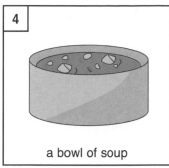 a bowl of soup	**5**  I'm not having soup.	**6**  Neither am I.
7 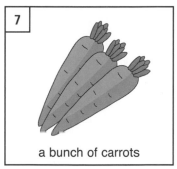 a bunch of carrots	**8**  I like carrots.	**9**  So do I.
10 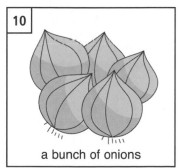 a bunch of onions	**11**  I don't like onions.	**12**  Neither do I.

13  She can swim.

14 I can't swim. Neither can I.

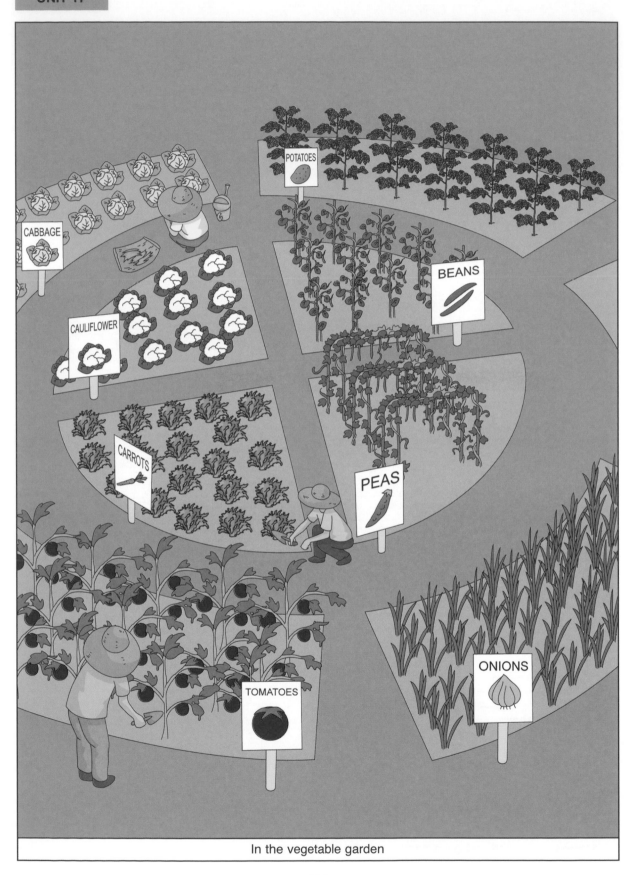

In the vegetable garden

1

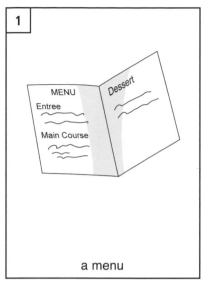

a menu

2

We had dinner at a restaurant last night. The service was very slow.

3

We ordered at 7 o'clock.

4

The entrée was served at 8 o'clock.

5

The main courses were served at 9.30.

6

We didn't have dessert until 11 o'clock.

7

I won't go there again.

Neither will I.

1

Which restaurant do you recommend?

2

I think this one is the best.

3

Do I need to book a table?

Yes, you'd better.

I'll do it now.

4

I'd like to book a table for four at 7.30, please.

5

I'm hungry.

You'd better eat an apple.

6

7

I'm not hungry now.

8

I'm thirsty.

You'd better drink some water.

9
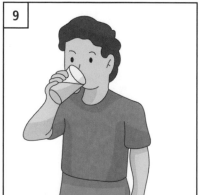

10

I'm not thirsty now.

1

It's raining here.

2

It's raining there.

3

It's raining everywhere.

4

Hello Jack.

5

Hello Mandy.

6

Hello everyone.

7

Put this in the suitcase.

8

Put that in the suitcase.

9

Put everything in the suitcase.

The Bensons

UNIT 18: If I won, I'd buy a new car.

In this unit you will learn the following:

- How to make conditional predictions
- How to talk about frequency

Here are the words you will learn to use:

always	empty	never	rarely
can't	full	often	sometimes

Here are some phrases you will learn to use:

as ... as	If I won . . . .
If I win . . .	If I'd won . . .

Grammar tips:
The new structures in this unit are conditionals and adverbs of frequency.

Here are some sentences you will practice:

Mick's tree is taller than Nick's.

He wasn't hungry, so he didn't eat it all.

If he'd been hungry, he would have eaten it.

If Louise won again she'd be very happy.

I rarely win.

a bowl

The bowl is empty.

The bowl is full.

a boy

I'm hungry.

I'm full.

1

Mick's tree is taller than Nick's.

2

Nick's tree is getting taller.

3

Nick's tree is as tall as Mick's.

4

Nick's tree is taller than Mick's.

5

6

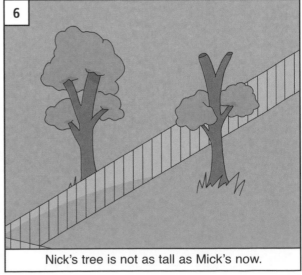

Nick's tree is not as tall as Mick's now.

1

If Paul wins again, he'll get another trophy.

2

If Linda always won,
she'd have as many trophies as Paul.

3

If Tex won again, he'd get another trophy.

4

If Louise won again, she'd be very happy.

5

If Phil won a race, he'd get his first trophy.

6

If George had won some races,
he'd have some trophies.

The Bensons

UNIT 19: I wish I could play the piano.

In this unit you will learn the following:

- How to express wishes
- How to congratulate people
- How to say goodbye

Here are the words you will learn to use:

accept	badly	change	immediately	lottery	piano	team	violinist
apply	celebrate	congratulations	interview	pianist	report	violin	wish

Here are some phrases you will learn to use:

well done	as soon as possible	job advertisement
good luck	go out	
bad luck	just a moment	

Here are some sentences you will practice:

He applied for the job.
I need the August sales report.
When can you start?
I wish I had a big car.

I wish I could play the piano well.
I play the piano badly.
I'd like to change my flight.

Grammar tips:
The new structures in this unit are adjectives and adverbs.

Rory saw an interesting job advertisement.

He applied for the job.

He went to the interview.

He got the job.

When can you start?

I can start next week.

He accepted the job.

I got the job.

He told his wife.

Congratulations. Well done!

He had a party to celebrate his new job.

good luck

bad luck

a lottery ticket

a team

The Bensons

1. carrot
2. ....
3. ....
4. ....
5. ....
6. ....
7. ....
8. ....
9. ....
10. ....
11. ....
12. ....
13. ....
14. ....
15. ....
16. ....
17. ....
18. ....

A

1. Is your shirt too big?

2. I'll have a coffee, thanks.

3. Which way to the bank?

4. Your jeans look good.

a. That way.

b. Yes, but they're too short.

c. No, it's just right.

d. That's a dollar fifty.

B

1. He likes going to the movies.

2. I don't like cold weather.

3. They're not swimming today.

4. She can't speak French.

5. I'll have some fish.

6. I won't have an entrée.

a. So will I.

b. So does she.

c. Neither will I.

d. Neither can they.

e. Neither do I.

f. Neither are we.

C

1. I'm hungry.

2. I'm thirsty.

3. I'd like a hamburger.

4. I'd like some soup.

5. When should we leave?

a. I'd like some too.

b. As soon as possible.

c. You'd better eat something.

d. I'd like one too.

e. You'd better drink something.

D

1. When will you be back?

2. Can I try them on?

3. I've lost fifty dollars.

4. My job interview is this afternoon.

a. Bad luck.

b. Good luck.

c. Yes, of course.

d. In five minutes.

| try | think | cost | take | too | reduction | would | for | better |

1 This one looks good.

It does. You'd better try it on.

2 Excuse me. I'd like to .... this on.

Of course. You can try it on over there.

3 What do you .... ?

I like it, but the trousers are .... long.

4 We can shorten them .... you.

Good. How much would that .... ?

5 That .... be twenty dollars extra.

And how much is the suit?

6 That one's on special. If you buy it today you'll get a 20% ....

7 How long will it .... to shorten the trousers?

A week.

8 OK. I'll take it.

was   So   full   I   enough   afraid   some   delicious   instead   have

1 Who'd like .... soup?

Yes, please.

2 Does it .... tomato in it?

Yes, it does.

I'm sorry. I'm ....
I don't eat tomato.

3 Oh. Would you like some
bread and cheese .... ?

Yes, thanks.

4 Could I have some
more soup? It's ....

Thank you.

5 Would you like some
more bread and cheese?

No thanks. I'm ....
It was very nice.

6 Has everyone had ....

I'd like some more.

.... would I.

No thanks. I've
had enough.

So have
....

7 That ....
lovely.

Yes, it was. Sorry
about the tomato.

That's alright.

181

until   day   would   if   appointment   change   next

1

Amherst Medical Center. Can I help you?

Hello. This is Wendy Jones. I have an .... with Doctor Spelling this afternoon. I'm afraid I have to .... it.

2

OK. When would you like to see him?

Well, Friday morning .... be good.

3

He's got appointments all .... on Friday. Would .... Monday afternoon be alright, after four o'clock?

Earlier would be better.

4

I'm afraid the doctor's busy .... four. The next appointment would be at nine on Tuesday morning.

I think that'll be OK. I'll have to check. Can I call you back?

5

That's fine. It would be good .... you could call back this morning.

Sure.

6

Thanks.

No problem.

before	again	everything	if	haven't	So	soon

1

It was lovely to meet you. We've really enjoyed it here.

.... have we. It's a pity you can't stay longer.

2

Yes. I hope we'll see you in New York.

Thanks. You've got our address .... you?

Yes, we have.

3

And .... you come to Sydney, you can stay with us.

That would be great.

4

We'll have to leave .... The taxi will be here in a few minutes.

OK. Are you sure we've packed .... ?

5

Yes. I checked .... we left the room.

We'd better go. The taxi's arrived.

6

Goodbye. Hope to see you .... soon.

Goodbye.

➤ shoes small these too Are

➤ right just they're No

➤ the long skirt too Is

➤ it's short too No

➤ big The jacket's too

➤ size I'll smaller get a

➤ is This small too

➤ larger a get I'll size

➤ coffee don't I want

➤ I Neither do

➤ long I talk for can't

➤ can Neither I

1

➤ go to have I soon

➤ do we So

2

➤ go We movie that to won't

➤ we will Neither

3

➤ coke I'd a like

➤ too one like I'd

4

➤ time party is What the

➤ thirty Seven

5

➤ need you do a When flight

➤ possible soon As as

6

➤ back you When be will

➤ two hours In

Answers to Unit 20

Unit 20, page 178

1. carrot	5. cabbage	9. sheep	13. plate	17. team
2. onion	6. cauliflower	10. pig	14. bowl	18. interview
3. beans	7. tomato	11. fish	15. piano	
4. peas	8. cow	12. swim	16. violin	

Unit 20, page 179

A. 1c 2d 3a 4b   B. 1b 2e 3f 4d 5a 6c   C. 1c 2e 3d 4a 5b   D. 1d 2c 3a 4b

Unit 20, page 180

1. better   2. try   3. think, too   4. for, cost   5. would   6. reduction   7. take

Unit 20, page 181

1. some   2. have, afraid   3. instead   4. delicious   5. full   6. enough, So, I   7. was

Unit 20, page 182

1. appointment, change   2. would   3. day, next   4. until   5. if

Unit 20, page 183

1. So   2. haven't   3. if   4. soon, everything   5. before   6. again

Unit 20, page 184

1. Are these shoes too small?
   No, they're just right.

2. Is the skirt too long?
   No, it's too short.

3. The jacket's too big.
   I'll get a smaller size.

4. This is too small.
   I'll get a larger size.

5. I don't want coffee.
   Neither do I.

6. I can't talk for long.
   Neither can I.

Unit 20, page 185

1. I have to go soon.
   So do we.

2. We won't go to that movie.
   Neither will we.

3. I'd like a coke.
   I'd like one too.

4. What time is the party?
   Seven thirty.

5. When do you need a flight?
   As soon as possible.

6. When will you be back?
   In two hours.

Answers to practice pages

Unit 1, page 7

1.	father	5. sister-in-law	9. daughter	13. sister	17. niece
2.	daughter	6. father	10. cousin	14. cousin	18. brother-in-law
3.	brother	7. daughter-in-law	11. uncle	15. grandfather	
4.	grandmother	8. brother	12. aunt	16. nephew	

Unit 7, page 66

4. Mum says <u>I can't go out</u>, because <u>it's raining</u>.

5. Mum says <u>I have to tidy my bedroom</u>, so <u>I can't go to the park</u>.

6. <u>We have to go now</u>, because <u>it's after ten o'clock</u>.

Unit 8, page 70

The flight <u>starts</u> at eleven o'clock and <u>finishes</u> at seven o'clock.

Unit 9, page 79

12. <u>Behind</u> the sofa.   14. <u>Beside</u> the TV.   16. <u>On</u> the table.

13. <u>In front of</u> his house.   15. <u>Under</u> the bed.

Unit 9, page 80

7. He <u>will</u> lift it.   8. He <u>won't</u> lift it.   9. He <u>might</u> lift it.

Unit 9, page 81

4. Yes.   5. No.   6. Maybe.

Unit 11, page 102

On the bed.   On the chair.   On the table.   In the wardrobe.   On the dresser.

Unit 14, page 123

4. Would you <u>lend me</u> your scarf, please?   5. I'd like to <u>borrow</u> $80,000, please.

8. He said he <u>doesn't have enough money to buy a car</u>, so <u>will have to rent one</u>.

Unit 16, page 146

4.1. I've got two cars.   4.2. One of them is new.   4.3. The other one is old.

Unit 19, page 172

1. I wish <u>I was rich</u>.   2. I wish <u>I had a big house</u>.   3. I wish <u>I played the violin well</u>.

Unit 19, page 177

12. <u>Goodbye</u>.

Grammar/Function/Topic in Volumes 1 and 2

Index for Volumes 1 and 2

aren't 1.4
arm 1.11
around 2.4
around the corner 1.12
arrive 1.8
arrive at 2.1
art gallery 1.2
as ... as 2.18
as soon as possible 2.19
ask 1.17
at 1.12
attendant 2.7
August 1.8
aunt 2.1
baby 1.4
back (n) 1.11
back (adj) 2.3
backache 1.11
backyard 2.3
bad 1.9
bad luck 2.19
bag 1.6
balcony 2.3
banana 1.6
band aid 2.13
bandage 2.13
bank 1.14
basketball player 1.9
bathroom 2.3
battery 2.14
beach 1.2
beans 1.9
beautiful 1.4
because 2.7
bedroom 2.3
beef 2.17
beep 1.17
before 1.14, 1.17
behind 2.9
bell 2.2
bench 2.12
beside 2.9
big 1.9
bill 1.11
bird 2.3
birthday 2.4
bite 2.13
black 1.14
block 2.4
blue 1.14
book 1.1
bored 2.2
boring 1.9
borrow 2.14
bottle of ... 1.6
bottom 2.8
bottom drawer 2.11
bowl 2.17
box 1.13
boxer 2.9
bra 2.11
branch 2.8

bread 1.9
breakfast 1.17
bring 1.2
broccoli 1.9
brother 1.1
brother-in-law 2.1
brown 1.14
bruised 2.13
bunch 2.17
burger 1.6
burnt 2.11
bus 1.8
bus stop 1.14
businessman 1.7
busy 1.17
but 1.2
butter the toast 2.1
buy 1.16
by 1.8
Bye. 1.11
cabbage 1.9
cake 1.6
call 1.12
camera 1.1
can 1.2
Can I help you? 1.9
can of ... 1.6
Can you tell me the time
    please? 1.18
Can you tell me when to
    get off? 1.19
can't 2.18
cap 1.9
car 1.1
car park 1.14
card 1.12
careful 2.13
careless 2.13
carrot 1.9
carton 1.13
cash 1.13
cat 2.1
cauliflower 1.9
caution 2.13
ceiling 1.13
celebrate 2.19
cent 1.8
centimetre 2.14
chair 2.1
change (vb) 2.19
change (n) 1.19
channel 2.6
cheap 1.9
check (vb) 2.2
chemist 1.13
cheque 2.14
chess 1.17
chest 2.13
chest of drawers 2.11
child 1.6
chips 1.6
chocolate bar 2.4

cinema 1.14
clean 1.16
clear the table 2.1
clock 1.18
close (adj) 2.9
close (v) 1.16
cloudy 2.6
coat 2.11
coffee 1.6
cold 1.4
colleague 1.3
comb 2.7
come 1.2
come back 2.7
comedy 2.6
comfortable 2.12
computer 2.6
concert 1.2
congratulations 2.19
cookie 1.6
corner 1.12
cough 2.13
Could you repeat that
    please? 1.7
cousin 2.1
cow 2.17
crawl 2.9
creased 2.11
credit card 1.13
crutches 2.13
cucumber 1.9
cup of ... 1.6
cut 2.13
cute 1.4
Dad 1.11
damage 2.14
danger 2.13
daughter 1.1
daughter-in-law 2.1
day 1.4, 1.8, 1.11
December 1.8
delicious 2.17
dentist 2.12
depart from 2.1
deposit 2.14
dessert 2.17
did 1.7
dining room 2.3
dinner 1.2, 1.17
dirty 1.16
disappointed 2.6
discount 2.14
dishwasher 2.6
distance 2.14
divided by 2.14
do 1.4
do the dishes 2.6
Do you have ...? 1.13
Do you like ...? 1.9
Do you take ...? 1.13
doctor 1.7
does 1.4

Does this bus go to? 1.19
doesn't 1.4
doesn't work 2.11
dollar 1.8
don't 1.4
done up 2.12
door 1.2
double bed 2.3
downstairs 2.3
dress (n) 2.11
dress (vb) 2.11
dresser 2.11
drill 2.14
drink 1.17
drive 1.16
driver's licence 2.14
drugstore 1.13
DVD 2.6
each 2.3
ear 1.11
earache 1.11
early 1.18
eat 1.16
egg 1.13
eight 1.6
eighteen 1.8
eighth 1.14
eighty 1.12
either 2.11
elephant 2.8
eleven 1.8
email 2.1
empty 1.17
enough 2.3
enter 1.2
entrée 2.17
entry 2.7
envelope 2.1
equal 2.3
evening 1.11
every 2.2
everyone 1.8
everything 2.17
everywhere 2.17
excellent 2.4
exchange 2.14
excited 2.2
exciting 2.2
Excuse me. 1.1
exercise 2.13
exit 1.2
expensive 1.9
express 2.7
extra 2.8
eye 2.13
eyelash 2.7
face 2.7
fall 2.11
family 1.1
far 2.9
fast 1.4
father 1.1

mouth 2.13
move 2.12
movie 2.6
multiplied by 2.14
Mum 1.16
mushroom 1.9
must be 2.11
my 1.1
My name's... 1.1
myself 2.11
name 1.1
narrow 1.9
near 1.12
need 1.13
neighbour 1.3
neither 2.17
nephew 2.1
never 2.2
new 1.13
news 2.6
newsagent 2.7
newspaper 1.17
next door 1.12
next to 1.12
niece 2.1
night 1.11
nine 1.6
nineteen 1.8
ninety 1.12
ninth 1.14
no 1.1
No parking. 1.19
No problem. 1.13
No, I haven't. 1.3
No, thanks. 1.6
nose 2.13
not 1.4
not ... enough 2.9
not enough 2.3
November 1.8
now 1.7
number 1.17
nurse 1.7
nuts 1.6
o'clock 1.18
occupation 1.7
October 1.8
off 2.1
often 2.18
OK 1.2
old 1.13
on 1.12, 2.1, 2.9
on time 2.2
once 2.2
one 1.6
one hundred 1.12
onion 1.9
open (v) 1.16
open (adj) 2.9
operation 2.8
opposite 1.12
or 1.13

orange 1.6, 1.14
order 2.17
other 2.16
our 1.1
ourselves 2.11
out 1.2
out of 2.3
over 2.9
over there 2.16
p.m. 1.18
pack 2.12
page 2.1
pair of 2.16
pair of sunglasses 1.9
panel beater 2.14
pants 1.9
parcel 2.1
park 1.19
party 1.2
pass the milk 2.1
past 1.14
pasta 1.9
path 2.3
pay 1.11
peach 1.6
pear 1.6
peas 1.9
pen 1.1
percent 2.14
petrol station 1.14
phone 1.17
pianist 2.19
piano 1.13
picnic 1.2
piece of ... 1.6
pig 2.17
plane 1.4
plane crash 2.6
plate 2.17
platform 2.7
play 1.4, 1.13
please 1.17
plum 1.6
plus 2.14
point 2.14
police officer 1.7
police station 1.12
pork 2.17
possibly 2.9
post office 1.14
postcard 2.1
postman 2.1
potato 2.17
pouch 2.8
powder 2.7
prescription 2.13
price 2.16
printer 2.6
probably 2.9
pull 1.16
purse 1.1
push 1.16

put 2.1
put on 2.13
quarter 1.18
quickly 2.1
race 2.9
radio 2.6
railway station 1.14
rain 2.6
rarely 2.18
rash 2.13
read 1.17
ready 2.7
receptionist 1.7
recommend 2.17
red 1.14
refund 2.14
registration number 2.14
remember 2.7
remote control 2.6
rent 2.14
report 2.19
rest 2.13
restaurant 1.2
return 2.7
rice 1.9
right (not wrong) 2.2
right (not left) 1.14
ring (the bell) 2.2
road 1.12
roof 1.14
room 1.13
room service 2.9
run 1.4
sad 1.18
safe 2.12
sale 2.16
sales assistant 1.7
same 2.16
sandwich 1.6
Saturday 1.8
sauce 2.3
sausage 1.6
saw (n) 2.14
say 2.2
scarf 2.14
school 1.8
scratch 2.13
seal 2.8
seat 1.4
second 1.14, 1.19
secretary 1.3
See you later. 1.11
sell 1.16
send a letter 2.1
separate 2.8
September 1.8
serve 2.17
service 2.17
seven 1.6
seventeen 1.8
seventh 1.14
seventy 1.12

share (with) 2.3
she 1.2
shed 2.3
sheep 2.17
shirt 2.11
shoe 1.4
shop 1.17
short 1.9, 1.17
shoulder 1.11
show 2.13
showers 2.6
sign 2.14
signature 2.14
since 1.8
single 2.7
single bed 2.3
sister 1.1
sister-in-law 2.1
sit 1.4
six 1.6
sixteen 1.8
sixth 1.14
sixty 1.12
size 2.16
skirt 2.11
sleep 1.16
slowly 1.7
small 1.9
snow 2.6
so 2.7
sock 1.6
sofa 2.1
soft 2.6
some 1.6
something to drink 1.6
something to eat 1.6
sometimes 2.2
somewhere 2.4
son 1.1
son-in-law 2.1
soon 2.13
Sorry. 1.11
Sorry, I can't. 1.2
soup 2.17
speak 1.17
special 2.16
sport 2.6
stadium 1.14
stamp 2.1
stand 2.9
stars 1.11
start 2.8
stay in bed 2.13
still 1.8
stockings 2.11
stomach 1.11
stomach ache 1.11
stop 1.11
stop smoking 2.13
storm 2.6
straight ahead 1.14
street 1.12